THE QUICK AND THE DEAD

RU-486 and the
New Chemical Warfare
Against Your Family

THE
QUICK
AND THE
DEAD

RU-486 and the
New Chemical Warfare
Against Your Family

George Grant

CROSSWAY BOOKS • WHEATON, ILLINOIS
A DIVISION OF GOOD NEWS PUBLISHERS

The Quick and the Dead.

Copyright © 1991 by George Grant.

Published by Crossway Books, a division of
Good News Publishers, 1300 Crescent Street, Wheaton, Illinois 60187.

Cover design: Dennis Hill

First printing, 1991

ISBN: 0-89107-664-6

Printed in the United States of America

Unless otherwise noted, all Scripture quotations are either the author's
own translations or are from the *New King James Version* of the Bible,
copyright © 1984 by Thomas Nelson, Inc., Nashville, Tennessee.

99		98		97		96		95		94		93		92	
15	14	13	12	11	10	9	8	7	6	5	4	3	2		

To my Uz
whom I love though in Heaven
and
to my Jz
whom I love though on earth

Christ is seated
At the right hand of the Father
And will come again to judge
The quick and the dead

TABLE OF CONTENTS

ACKNOWLEDGMENTS

Currente Calamo[1]

No other success in life—not being President, or being wealthy, or going to college, or anything else—comes up to the success of the man and woman who can feel that they have done their duty and that their children and grandchildren rise up to call them blessed.[2]

THEODORE ROOSEVELT

If this were a regular sermon preached from a pulpit, of course I should make it long and dismal, like a winter's night, for fear people should call me eccentric. As it is only meant to be read at home, I will make it short, though it will not be sweet, for I have not a sweet subject.[3]

CHARLES H. SPURGEON

S AMUEL Taylor Coleridge often asserted that material is borrowed from writer to writer and from generation to generation, "in a series of immitated immitations—shadows of shadows of shadows of a farthing candle placed between two looking glasses."[4] Centuries before, Solomon said it another way:

ix

"There is nothing new under the sun" (Ecclesiastes 1:9). In the case of both this book and its subject matter, that is certainly true.

Now to be sure, the technologies discussed here are of a relatively recent vintage. And my prose has only just now been composed. Nevertheless, each shares a heritage—a heritage of intractable conflict and controversy—tracing back to time immemorial. As a result, I have freely relied on the thinking, the wisdom, the conceptions, and the counsel of many others—particularly those who have gone on before me in the battle for life and liberty.

My friends in Europe—especially Paul de Forte, Emil Allande, and Michelle Gallion in France, and Sir Fred Catherwood, Jenny Rosser, and Louise Whitbread in England—helped tremendously in making my visits to their countries pleasant, fruitful, and informative.

In the United States, David Dunham at Legacy Communications, Carol Everett at Marketplace Christian Network, and Bill Breslin at Coral Ridge Ministries have all ungrudgingly offered help and encouragement to me at every turn. In addition, my remarkable staff—Mary Jane Morris, Mark Horne, Jennifer Burkett, Susan Allen, Nancy Britt, Charles Wolfe, Jim Small, and Carol Sue Quarquesso—all served faithfully in thankless tasks through many difficult days.

Luc Nadeau salvaged much of the text of this book—laboring for many long hours and using his mondo cyberspace magic—after my longtime collaborator Mac N. Tosh decided to go out to lunch never to return. And Angie Gaines saved me many hours by entering and reentering mounds of data following that calamitous event.

My publishers, Lane and Jan Dennis in the United States and Christopher Catherwood in the United Kingdom, believed in the importance of this project despite the conventional publishing industry wisdom that "issues books" simply are not economically viable.

I had the great pleasure of chatting with Steve and Annie Chapman in the airport in Wichita—after we had participated together in one of the most remarkable demonstrations of the breadth and depth of the pro-life movement, right there in the heartland. I was thrilled—I'd been a fan since the days of Dogwood. They promised to send my daughter some of their latest music. And they did. But I have to confess that it was Dad who wore the tapes out—during the writing of this book. I don't know whether to thank them or to rail against them for the innumerable times I had to abandon the keyboard to laugh or cry or pray or ponder. The rest of the soundtrack was ably provided by Paul Overstreet, Kathy Mattea, Gary Chapman, Bob Bennett, Michael Card, Charlie Peacock, Susan Ashton, and of course, the master interpreter of *joyeuse garde*, Kemper Crabb.

Once again my beloved family bore with my absences—both physical and mental—during the researching, writing, and editing stages. My wife, Karen, and my three children, Joel, Joanna, and Jesse, are a steadfast support for all that I am and all that I do.

> *As a fountain gushes forth its water,*
> *So my heart gushes forth the praise of the Lord,*
> *And my lips bring forth praise to Him.*

> *My tongue becomes sweet by His anthems,*
> *My hearing is suffused in his thunderous majesty,*
> *And my limbs are set to dancing by His odes.*
> *My face rejoices with exultation,*
> *And my spirit exults in love,*
> *My very nature radiates His glory.*

For in His graciousness,
He has given such as these to love me,
And hold me to close accounts.
All praise be to the living God on high.[5]

In the marvelous providence of God, I have indeed been surrounded by the goodness of others. For that I am both profoundly humbled and deeply grateful. To you all, I offer my sincerest thanks.

Dum Wichita est spes est.[6]

Feast of Cyril Lucarius
Lewes, East Sussex, England

INTRODUCTION

Finem Respice[1]

No abounding of material prosperity shall avail us if our
spiritual senses atrophy. The foes of our own household
will surely prevail against us unless there be in our
people an inner life which finds its outer expression in a
morality like unto that preached by the seers and
prophets of God when the grandeur that was Greece
and the glory that was Rome still lay in the future.[2]

THEODORE ROOSEVELT

I would have everybody able to read, and write, and
cipher; indeed I don't think a man can know too much;
but mark you, the knowing of these things is not
education; and there are millions of your reading and
writing people who are as ignorant as neighbor
Norton's calf, that did not know its own mother.[3]

CHARLES H. SPURGEON

OUR culture's tortured struggle over abortion has recently
taken a nasty turn with the introduction of several powerful new abortifacient drugs. Wildly heralded by feminist and pro-abortion groups, roundly denounced by Christian

and pro-life groups, the drugs have been drawn into the eye of a fierce storm of political intrigue, subversion, manipulation, and infighting.

Methotrexate, Epostane, Lilopristone, Onapristone, and Mifepristone all purport to be safe and effective post-coital "contraceptive methods" or "morning after pills." Thus they have been lauded by sundry war-weary politicians and journalists in both Europe and America as a possible peaceful compromise on the issue of abortion. No such luck. Though quickly embraced by the World Health Organization, the Population Council, Planned Parenthood International, and the United Nations Council on Population Affairs, multiplied revelations of disturbing risks, side effects, and complications plus serious questions about practical complexity and tangible effectiveness, along with unrelenting opposition by pro-life organizations and medical ethics associations, have thrown the drugs into a boiling caldron of ideology, technology, sociology, and theology.

This short book is by no means an attempt to sort out all the questions surrounding the development, application, and consumption of these drugs. Instead, it is simply designed to provide a cogent introduction to the issue so that concerned parents, teachers, counselors, doctors, lawyers, public officials, voters, and activists can make wise and informed decisions about them.

In this increasingly polarized and controversial environment, well-intended souls on both sides of the issue find themselves carried along by don't-confuse-me-with-the-facts rhetoric, while others—again from each end of the spectrum—feel that the facts are more important than their use. Hopefully this monograph will serve as a partial antidote to both of these lamentable tendencies.

———

The structure of the book is fairly straightforward.

In Part I, the personal and practical dimensions of these new "contraceptive" and "contragestational" technologies are established. Chapter One describes the experience of one woman who, wowed by the promise of the new drugs, actually submitted herself to the trying procedures.

In Part II, the roots of the growing pharmacological conflict are examined. Chapter Two is a recapitulation of the history and background of the drugs, focusing particularly on the most familiar of them, Mifepristone and Mifegyne—or RU-486 as it is commonly called. Chapter Three recounts the long search for simple abortifacients and examines the impulses that give rise to such a search. Chapter Four documents the changing nature of the omnipresent medical industry and probes its impact on family issues. Chapter Five examines the role of media demagoguery in this swirling controversy.

In Part III, tentative conclusions are drawn, opportunities are highlighted, and alternatives are explored. Chapter Six takes the wider view of our current place in the annals of history in order to help provide a clearer context for the issue as well as attempting to outline a practical agenda for the future.

———

It is only fair to state at the outset that this entire discussion is framed by certain basic presuppositions: that all men and women are created equal; that they are endowed by their Creator with certain inalienable rights; that those rights begin with the rights to life, liberty, and the pursuit of genuine happiness; and that to risk all for the sake of such freedoms is a moral imperative. In short, this book is forthrightly and unabashedly informed by the very same commitment to the orthodox verities of the Christian worldview that gave rise to the flowering of Western civilization in general and that gave impetus to the burgeoning of Western democratic republicanism in particular. It is only on that foundation, after all, that we can ever hope to bring resolution to the clash of perspectives that now threatens to wreck our great experiment in liberty on the shoals of division and derision.

If this book can in any way contribute to a confident return to that once indomitable consensus, it will have accomplished much.

Deo soli gloria. Jesu juva.[4]

PART I

BREEDING CONTEMPT

The world is at this moment passing through one of those terrible periods of convulsion when the souls of men and of nations are tried as by fire. Woe to the man or to the nation that at such a time stands as once Laodicea stood; as the people of ancient Meroz stood, when they dared not come to the help of the Lord against the mighty. In such a crisis the moral weakling is the enemy of the right, the enemy of life, liberty, and the pursuit of happiness.[1]

THEODORE ROOSEVELT

Those who know the world best, trust it least: those who trust it at all are far from wise; as well trust a horse's heel or a dog's tooth.[2]

CHARLES H. SPURGEON

1

Paris in Spring

Pallida Mars[3]

In securing any kind of peace, the first essential is to guarantee to every man the most elementary of rights: the right to his own life. Murder is not debatable.[4]
THEODORE ROOSEVELT

Do not choose your way by its looks alone: after all, handsome shoes often pinch the feet.[5]
CHARLES H. SPURGEON

THE fountains fall with hallowed delicacy into a framing space in the Place de la Concorde. Blue hues creep out from behind the Colonades in the Rue de Rivoli and through the grillwork of the Tuileries. The low elegant outlines of the Louvre are a serious metallic gray against the setting sun. Well-tended branches hang brooding over animated cafes, embracing conversations with tender intimacy. Long windows open onto iron-clad balconies in marvelously archaic hotels, while gauzy lace curtains flutter across imagined hopes and wishes and dreams. Romance wafts freely in the sweet cool breezes off the Seine.

Ah, Paris in spring.

There is nothing quite like it.

Meredith Alexander, like so many before her, found its allure completely irresistible. When she had the opportunity to participate in a foreign university studies program during her junior year, she jumped at the chance. "Who wouldn't want to study in the most exotic city in the world?" she asked. "I was ecstatic. My parents, though, were a bit apprehensive. Part of it was the money, the distance, and the cultural difference. But they were also concerned about me—about my emotional and spiritual maturity. I quickly allayed their fears. I told them there really was nothing to worry about. I could handle myself just fine. As it turns out, they were right, and I was wrong. Dead wrong."

Meredith went ahead and enrolled in the program, obtained a student's visa, made all the arrangements, and launched into the adventure of it all. She was even able to secure a small attic apartment just blocks away from the university campus in central Paris. "Really, everything seemed so perfect," she said. "Registration went off without a hitch—I got every one of the classes I was hoping for. And my apartment—well, I couldn't have possibly asked for anything better. It was in a wonderful eighteenth-century building replete with high ceilings, ornamented plaster bas-relief across one wall, huge shuttered windows, antique furniture, and loads of dusty old books. And to top it all off, it was incredibly inexpensive."

On her student's budget she couldn't afford the typical tourist's initiation to the city—sitting in the chic cafes along the Champs Elysees for hours sipping champagne at twelve dollars a glass, or buying leather at Louis Vuitton at a thousand dollars per garment, or snatching up two hundred dollar scarves at Hermes, or eating at the epicurean five-star Bristol Hotel at more than three hundred dollars a meal—but she threw herself into the Parisian lifestyle nonetheless.

Each day after her morning classes she would wander over to the Pont Neuf bridge to explore the wares of the *bouquinistes*— the traditional French booksellers who had pioneered their unique brand of transportable trade early in the seventeenth century. She would then visit one of the many magnificent museums or perhaps eat a picnic lunch in the Bois de Boulogne, the huge park along the city's western ridge. Often she would end up gawking at the jubilant carnival atmosphere at the Champs de Mars just below the Eiffel Tower.

Nowhere does the novelist's prose slip more readily into the bland tones of the travel guidebook. Paris is a marvel of vintage sensory delights. And Meredith drank deeply from its draft. The staccato sounds of the clicking of saucers in the Place de la Contrescarpe, the trumpeting of traffic around the Arch de Triumph, and the conspiratorial whispering on benches in the Jardin de Luxembourg seemed to play a jangling Debussy score in the twilight hours. The nostalgic smells of luxuriant perfumes, wine, and brandy; the invigorating odors of croissants, espresso, and cut lavender; and the acrid fumes of tobacco, roasted chestnuts, and salon fragrances seem to texture a sweet and subtle Monet upon the canvas of *l'entente de la vie*. The dominating sights of the yellow towers of Notre Dame, the arched bridges cutting across the satin sheen of the river, and the stately elegance of the Bourbon palaces and pavilions scattered about the city like caches of mercy seemed to sculpt a muscular Rodin bronze on the *tabla rasa* landscape.

"I was so free there," she said. "I felt unfettered and alive. Everything was so stimulating—it seemed that every day I could literally bathe in the greatest art, music, literature, and ideas mankind had ever conceived. It was almost Heaven."

Almost. But not quite.

Victor Hugo, who loved the city with a passion, warned that

the rich atmosphere of Parisian culture was deceptively intoxicating. He often asserted, "No one can spend any length of time in Paris without being captivated by satyrs or muses or cupids or bacchuses or all of them together."[6]

Meredith was captivated by all of them together.

Falling in with bohemian friends, she began to neglect her studies in order to devote herself to the delicacies of the flesh. "We'd go out on the town virtually every night," she told me, "hopping from one fashionably obscure cafe or bar to another. We'd be dancing, drinking, and philandering until the wee hours of the morning—and then I'd have to try to make it to my classes the next day. It wasn't long before I had become a real mess."

And then things took an odd turn for the worse: Meredith fell in love.

"At first, everything seemed to get better," she said. "I guess love really is blind. Marc came along right when I needed a change—some stability. He was so romantic—he perfectly fit my imagined stereotype of the gallant and chivalrous Frenchman. I fell head-over-heels in love almost immediately. The course the relationship ultimately took seems dully predictable from the vantage of hindsight, but at the time I was entirely taken by him."

Despite her best efforts at commitment, the relationship with Marc eventually turned sour. "I'll spare you the gory details, but suffice it to say that the moment I discovered I was pregnant, he became very, very scarce." Her voice had became a whisper. "Finally, one afternoon he stopped by the apartment and handed me an envelope stuffed with about two hundred and fifty dollars and a couple of brochures from local abortion clinics. He said good-bye, turned on his heel, and that was it. I haven't seen him since."

Frightened and alone, Meredith had no earthly idea which way to turn. She was emotionally paralyzed.

One afternoon a couple of days later she saw a shabby poster pasted to a campus kiosk advertising a "maternal help center." It promised "compassionate Christian alternatives to abortion" for women caught in "the throes of a crisis pregnancy." She jotted down the number and dropped it into her purse—and then promptly forgot about it. She had become convinced there were no real "alternatives" for her.

She agonized over her plight. She stopped eating. She lost weight. She could hardly sleep. She avoided all her old friends and haunts. Unable to stand the trauma any longer, she retrieved Marc's envelope and conjured up a deadly resolve: she would kill the unwanted child growing inside her womb. She would be done with the whole mess as quickly and as painlessly as possible and then get on with her life. "If I had only known then what I know now, things could have been so different," she later said. "I could have avoided so much grief."

One of the brochures in the envelope featured information about a new abortion procedure Meredith had heard a great deal about: RU-486 or Mifegyne. "It was supposed to be safe and easy," she remembered. "Just take a pill and *poof*, that's it. It's over. Kind of an at-home, do-it-yourself, private abortion."

She called the clinic and set up an appointment.

The prodigious building housing the clinic was built as a bedlam[7] more than a century ago, and became a prison, then again a lunatic asylum, and finally a hospital. It was converted into a government-run ambulatory care center during the Mitterand years of deprivatization and collectivization. It was a somber gothic institution—rising four stories to sharply pitched gables and slate roofs. It was an insolent impenetrable structure—like a continental dogma or a bureaucrat's humor.

According to state regulations, Meredith was required to submit to a comprehensive psychological analysis. "They said I was perfectly fine," she told me, "Which just goes to show you how little they know and how imprecise their science actually is."

After that, she had to talk with a "family planning" counselor. "That was really a joke," she admitted. "We didn't talk about *family* matters at all. We didn't talk about *planning*. And I certainly wouldn't call our conversation *counseling*. It was just an opportunity for the clinic to take care of a few technicalities—like signing a liability release form and an insurance waiver. I feel that if someone would have taken the time to talk to me, if only for a moment or two, I would have been able to make a more responsible decision. As it was, I was on an emotional runaway train, and the clinic staff merely added fuel to the fire." The counselor's words worked strange alchemy on her—like learning Latin from a parrot—and she relented.

The receptionist at the clinic scheduled Meredith to come back just over a week later—once the government-mandated waiting period had elapsed. At that time she would receive a prescribed abortifacient dose of Mifegyne.

It was a long walk home.

It was an even longer week afterwards. Meredith wrestled with plaguing doubt. She was tortured with second thoughts, qualms, and misgivings. She weighed all her pros and cons. She even prayed for the first time in years, hoping against hope that somehow, some way she could find a way to avoid the dastardly course she had set into motion.

The whole thing was turning out to be a lot more complicated than she had bargained on. RU-486 sounded frightfully dangerous, not safe. It appeared to be terribly difficult, not easy. It wasn't at all private. And as far as being an at-home, do-it-yourself procedure—well, that was the farthest thing from the reality she had discovered at the clinic.

Throughout the week she struggled fitfully with enigmas, mysteries, and anomalies of both heart and soul—her ambivalent vision skewed through one ravenous and one lenten eye.

The last evening before she was scheduled to go to the clinic, she left her apartment, crossed over to the Ile de la Cite and approached Notre Dame. She walked beside the great cathedral along the Rue de Cloitre. Its magnificence subsumed her in lofty thoughts of rapture and refreshment.

Architecture is a litmus test for the character of a culture. After all, the most valuable things in any human society are those very permanent and irrevocable things—things like families. And architecture comes nearer to being very permanent and irrevocable than any other man-made craft simply because it is so difficult to dispose of. A book may be torn to pieces, a painting may be hidden in a closet, a symphony may be ignored, but a spire flung toward Heaven poses procedural difficulties to all but the most fiercely determined suppressors.

According to the great medieval builder and designer Michel di Giovanni:

> Church architecture ought to be an earthly and temporal fulfillment of the Savior's own prophecy that though the voices of men be still, the rocks and stones themselves will cry out with the laud and praise and honor due unto the King of kings and the Lord of lords.[8]

One look at Notre Dame—or virtually any cathedral in Europe for that matter—and it becomes readily apparent that in spite of all other possible shortcomings, medieval Parisians clearly comprehended that mandate. Taking their cue from the vast treasury of Biblical symbolism, those pioneers of Western culture left us a glorious heritage that continues to this day to translate sight into insight. Everything in the multifaceted design of the thirteenth-century cathedral towering over the Seine—whether consciously or unconsciously—reflected some profound theological conception. Towers, spires, buttresses, bells, porches, gargoyles, aisles, transepts, naves, chancels, vaults, ambulatories, stained-glass windows, sacristies, iconostasises, and narthexes were not simply pragmatic designations on a floor plan. They were integral aspects of the message those early congregants in Paris wished to convey.

But what struck Meredith as she stood there that night was that they were also entirely unnecessary. They were unnecessary because beauty is never *necessary*. It is never functional or useful, because beauty somehow transcends the categories of the pragmatic. As theologian Alexander Schmemann has said:

> When, expecting someone we love, we put a beautiful table-cloth on the table and decorate it with candles and flowers, we do all this not out of necessity, but out of love. As long as Christians love the Kingdom of God, and not only discuss it, they will represent it and signify it in art and beauty and theologically pregnant architecture.[9]

Scriptural teaching asserts that the Holy Spirit always establishes an environment of visible glory around the Throne of God—sometimes with clouds or flames, sometimes with angels or stars, sometimes with pure light or rainbows, and sometimes with burnished metals or precious stones. Historically, the architectural precedent seen in this remarkable glory environment—whether portrayed in the Garden of Eden, in Noah's Ark, in the desert Tabernacle, in the Temple, or in the New Heavens and New Earth—was taken to be the norm for church architecture. Since the glory environment proclaims the majesty of the Sovereign Lord, it made sense to those earlier Christians that the environment of the church should proclaim it as well. They believed their churches should be Biblical and that they should be simultaneously beautiful—going beyond the necessary. They believed, in other words, that the rocks and stones themselves should cry out, "Hosanna to the King."

Meredith saw all that and more. She wondered what it must have been like to have faith like that—culture-transforming faith. And she wondered if such faith could ever again exist in this poor fallen world.

Before she left the cloisters, she spent a long while looking up at the sturdy and stalwart statue of Charlemagne guarding the narthex of the cathedral. His fierce countenance seemed terribly dark and foreboding. A sudden wave of fear snapped the spell of sanctity she had felt earlier, and with a shudder she crossed over to the other side of the street. She turned left up the Quai aux Fleurs and started for home, exhausted. Just a half a block up though, at the site of Canon Fulbert's twelfth-century house, she stopped again. There she read, for what must have been the hundredth time, a weathered bronze plaque dedicated to the memory of Paris's two most celebrated lovers: Abelard and Heloise.

Behind her now was Notre Dame. Before her was the canon's home. The juxtaposition was poignant: the house of God, that of the devil, and her wandering between the two. She had become like Abram, she thought, camped between Bethel and Ai—but without his faith.

Peter Abelard was a profoundly brilliant and immensely popular university lecturer during the halcyon days of the early twelfth century. His imposing intellect, stunning good looks, and winsome personality made him the focus of popular fashion—the medieval equivalent of a celebrity. But he was a celebrity of real substance—unlike today's warholian paroxysms. His pioneering synthesis of Christian dogma and Greek philosophy—focusing particularly on the philosophical interaction between Aristotle, Plato, and the Patristics—greatly influenced his renowned pupils Peter Lombard, John of Salisbury, and Arnold of Brescia, and even anticipated the work of Thomas Aquinas two generations later. Though he was often opposed in his views by formidable rivals such as Bernard of Clairveaux, Abelard was clearly a giant in the land.

Heloise was the stunningly beautiful niece of the stern canon of Notre Dame. Though but a teen, she became the object of Abelard's attentions—and ultimately his passions. After convincing Fulbert to let him become the girl's tutor, he seduced her, and she conceived a son.

The two lovers were subsequently married, but Fulbert's wrath could not be appeased. He continually harassed and threatened them both. In desperation, Abelard attempted to secretly remove his young wife and son to the safety of a convent in Argenteuil. Thinking Abelard planned to abandon her there, the outraged Fulbert had a band of ruffians attack and emasculate him.

The tragic story ends with Abelard in a monastery, Heloise in a convent, and their son, Astrolabe, raised as an oblate in a nearby hermitage—their family, their love, and their lives completely shattered.

Meredith clutched the relevance of history like a rag doll to her breast—and she felt more isolated and alone than ever. More often than not, reality is better represented by a dime-store novel than by a *missa solemnis*. For all their beauty and brilliance, Abelard and Heloise were bound by the same fussy philistine chains that bound her. For all their passion and pathos, they were forced to follow the same monotonous sequentiality of a sin-scarred life. She had always been prone to wander into other peoples' dreams, never to find her way back. So now she swallowed hard and accepted *their* fate as her own.

Doubling back, she crossed over to the Ile St. Louis. She leaned over the wooden rail of the bridge and looked up the river to the glittering lights of the city. Mingling with her tears, the water below was as smooth as Parisian silk and as black as Norman coal. As a couple walked past arm in arm, a *bateau mouche* went by, all bright with lights, going fast and quiet up and out of sight under the bridge. Still, it seemed that all the world had gone dark as medieval silhouettes clawed high against the sky and ancient trees shrouded the streets in ominous shadows.

She recalled Cyril Connolly's familiar lonely oeuvre:

> The city strains at her moorings, the river eddies round the stone prow where tall poplars stand like masts, and mist rises about the decaying houses which seventeenth century nobles raised on their meadows. Yielding asphalt, sliding waters; long windows with iron bars set in damp walls; anguish and fear. Rendez-vous des Mariniers, Hotel de Lauzun: moment of the night when the saint's blood liquefies, when the leaves shiver and presentiments of loss stir within the dark coil of our fatality.[10]

Finally, with tears still burning in her eyes, she returned home for a long night of fitful sleep. Her vigil had ended.

The next morning, she rose early. The hesitation and wonderment of the previous evening were gone but not forgotten. A wave of morning sickness swept over her as she descended the steep staircase in her apartment building. Even so, she remained undeterred. She had well-worn calluses on her thoughts. Nothing could erode her resolve now—not the profundities of history or the profanities of modernity. Her course was set.

The city seemed even more austere and distant than the pale morning sky as she walked toward her appointment. She was torn between thinking that the world is wild and full of marvels and that it is dull and altogether routine—as if either could make a difference in this moment which was as exaggerated as eulogy.

In the half-light of dawn, the clinic appeared to be a grotesque samba tattoo on the landscape—a semi-nocturnal image that had haunted her now for nearly a fortnight. But after only a moment's nervous hesitation, she approached the doors. She did not enter at the front like a visitor; instead, she crept around to the back like a traitor.

And then she went in.

The clinic staff was ready for her. They ushered her into a small examining room and had her sign two more legal documents—a one-page release form and a government information inquiry. A few moments later a midwife carrying a small blue suitcase entered the small room and introduced herself. She then briefly explained how RU-486 actually worked. She spoke of "receptors" and "anti-hormones" and "steroid down-regulators" and "progesterone actions" in lucid happy tones. But Meredith was hardly paying attention. She just wanted it all over.

"Did you understand all that?" the woman asked her.

"Yes."

"Are you sure you want to go ahead then?"

"Yes."

"There is no turning back once you've taken the drug."

"I know. No turning back."

The midwife unlocked the suitcase and took out a sealed blue-and-white pharmaceutical box and handed it to Meredith.

Meredith's hand trembled. Her eyes welled. She emptied the sole contents of the box—three small pills—into her hand. She clenched her teeth and set her jaw with determination.

"OK. I'm gonna do it. I'm gonna do it."

The woman handed her a glass of water.

Meredith took the glass in her left hand and looked down at the pills in her right hand. They were about the size and the color of aspirin.

One by one she put them into her mouth and washed them

down with the water. After the third swallow she took a long deep breath.

"It is done. And I did it myself."

"Yes, dear. You did it. It's almost over."

"I did it. I killed my child."

"Now, now, don't say such things. It's OK. You'll be fine. It's almost over."

But of course it really wasn't OK, she really wasn't fine, and it really wasn't almost over. Not by a long shot.

She closed her eyes and shuddered with remorse.

It was just beginning. And she knew that only too well.

After she rested for a few moments, the midwife told Meredith she could go home. The drug would do its work, she was assured in soothing tones, but it would be about forty-eight hours before the bleeding would begin—bleeding that would indicate the abortion had been successful. At that time she would have to return to the clinic to take a dose of prostaglandin—a powerful labor-inducing drug—so any remains of her unwanted pregnancy could be flushed out of her body.

"Two days!" she later exclaimed. "Two days were an eternity. What was supposed to be a quick and easy private procedure had somehow evolved into a prolonged nightmare."

But even after those two days the waiting was not done.

When she returned to the clinic at the prescribed time, the midwife expressed mild surprise that a menses flow had not yet begun. But she comforted and consoled Meredith, then said everything would be just fine nonetheless and gave her the prostaglandin injection.

After a couple of hours, Meredith—exhausted and frightened now—began to feel a few irregular uterine contractions. But still there was no menses. The midwife told her there was nothing to be concerned about—the expulsion would certainly occur sometime in the next four or five days. And with that she dispatched her home again. That night Meredith began to have severe contractions. She was wracked with nausea, dizziness, diarrhea, and vomiting. Eventually the pain became so intense she could barely even get out of bed to use the bathroom. Hour after hour she writhed in agony.

"I honestly just wanted to die. And I thought I actually might at any moment. My breathing became labored, and my heart was racing. The abdominal pain was unbearable. Even my vision had become blurred."

After three miserable days and nights of anguish, she screwed up enough resolve to make her way down the hall to the phone. She called for an ambulance. When the paramedics arrived, she was unconscious, sprawled on the floor in a pool of blood.

For the next seven days the hospital worked to repair the damage to Meredith's fragile health.

"They said I was one of the rare exceptions," she told me. "Very lucky. After the initial examination in the emergency room, the doctors recognized immediately that I was a victim of a failed pharmaceutical abortion. They were forced to perform a surgical D & C and suction procedure right away. They stopped some internal hemorrhaging and gave me a transfusion—apparently I had lost a tremendous amount of blood. They attached me to a respirator, briefly, because my lungs had begun to fill with fluid. And they attached me to a renal filter because my kidneys had become very strained—the toxicity levels in my bloodstream were well above the acceptable range. There were also a number of serious cardiac irregularities they worried about for a while—but those seemed to disappear after a couple of days. I was a total mess. But I was also extremely lucky. I was alive. One nurse told me that was a minor miracle in and of itself. I thought about that a lot. I began to believe it was true."

It is said there are only two ways of getting home. One is to never leave it. The other is to travel round the whole world till you return to it. Meredith—like so many prodigals before her—had tried the circuitous route. But now, at long last, she was on the return leg of the journey.

Shortly after she was dismissed from the hospital, she noticed a small slip of paper under the corner of a table in her apartment. She reached down and picked it up—a strange foreboding compelling her. It was a phone number scribbled in her own hand. Suddenly she remembered: the Christian maternal help center. The note must have fallen out of her purse weeks ago.

For some unknown reason she called the number. And her story gushed out. For the first time she revealed all her shame, her remorse, her guilt, her pity, her pain, and her fears.

Over the next several days two counselors from the center took turns nursing Meredith's shattered emotions. They cooked meals for her. They tidied up the apartment. They ran a few errands and took care of some unresolved details at the university. But mostly they just listened to her.

And so she began to heal.

"My recovery was doubly difficult because not only did my body have to mend, my soul had to mend as well," she said. "I had to come to terms with what I had done—to myself and to my child. If I had gotten a regular abortion, I might have been able to shift the blame, somehow, to Marc or to the doctor. But with RU-486, there was really no one to blame but myself. I was the one who made the decision. I was the one who took the pills. I did it. That is a terrible thing to have to face up to."

As soon as she was well enough to travel, Meredith bought a plane ticket home. She realized now that her parents had been right all along. On her last evening in Paris, she revisited some of her old haunts and was struck by their obvious sadness. For the first time she saw emptiness in the eyes of vast numbers of the denizens of

Gay Paree. The keen paradox of a simultaneous deep hollowness and shallow extravagance startled her. Here, she realized, nature is tame and civilization is wild.

A beautiful civilization can make a person either love beauty or take it utterly for granted. A free civilization can either encourage responsibility or smother it. A great civilization can either spark the flames of faith or snuff them out. A civilization is a terrible and unpredictable thing.

She walked toward the Pont au Change where the Seine forms a sort of pool traversed by a swift current. It is a place feared by boatmen—a lonely treacherous place. She leaned over the parapet and gazed into the rushing waters, recollecting the sum of her sorrows. It was that odd sepulchral moment that immediately precedes midnight—when the stars are cloaked in the clouds and not a light can be seen from the Cite—and not a passerby is at hand—only the faint gleam of distant traffic and the shadowy outlines of Notre Dame in one direction and Fulbert's house in the other.

At long last she took a deep cleansing breath and whispered a mournful French lament—a verse learned by rote during her school days—days that now seemed so very long ago:

> *J'etais la quand la chose s'est passee, a cote du Pont Neuf,*
> *Non loin du monument qu'on apple la Monnaie.*
> *J'etais la quand elle s'est penchee et c'est moi qui l'ai poussee.*
> *Il n'y avait rien d'autre a faire.*
> *Je suis la Misere.*
> *J'ai fait mon metier et la Seine a fait de meme,*
> *Quand elle a referme sur elle so bras fraternal.*[11]

And then she turned to leave—the wild civilization now behind her.

Ah, Paris in spring.

There is nothing quite like it.

PART II

A BITTER PILL

Progress has brought us both unbounded opportunities and unbridled difficulties. Thus, the measure of our civilization will not be that we have done much, but what we have done with that much. I believe that the next half century will determine if we will advance the cause of Christian civilization or revert to the horrors of brutal paganism. The thought of modern industry in the hands of Christian charity is a dream worth dreaming. The thought of industry in the hands of paganism is a nightmare beyond imagining. The choice between the two is upon us.[1]

THEODORE ROOSEVELT

They say you may praise a fool till you make him useful. I don't know much about that, but I do know that if I get a bad knife I generally cut my finger, and a blunt axe is far more trouble than profit. A handsaw is a good thing, but not to shave with.[2]

CHARLES H. SPURGEON

2

Death by Any Other Name

Res Ipsa Loquitur[3]

Never will I sit motionless while directly or indirectly apology is made for the murder of the helpless.[4]

THEODORE ROOSEVELT

The fox admires the cheese; if it were not for that he would not care a rap for the raven. The bait is not put into the trap to feed the mouse, but to catch him. We don't light a fire for the herring's comfort, but to roast him.[5]

CHARLES H. SPURGEON

IN the Place de la Bastille, there stands a triumphant column crowned with a gamboling figure. It marks the site where a Jacobin mob started a revolution and ended an age. It is a monument to the fact that the greatest part of human history has been symbolic.

The fact is that when it was liberated, the Bastille was not a horrible prison. It was hardly a prison at all. There were only seven inmates—and all of them were quite mad. There was but a single jailer and virtually no fortifications. It was a decrepit ruin.

But while the Bastille had long ceased to be an instrument of oppression, it was still very much a *symbol* of oppression. And like all men, the Jacobins had an unshakable instinct for symbols.

The liberation and destruction of the Bastille was thus not a radical reform. It was a religious iconoclasm. It was the breaking of a symbol. And because symbols are often the most powerful integrating forces in a culture, it was the breaking of a culture.

As in the French Revolution in the eighteenth century, the struggle over the sanctity of human life today is fraught with conflicting symbols and raging iconoclasm. And at the center of that semiotic conflict stands the RU-486 abortion drug.

RU-486 is actually not a terribly significant gynecological development—it is but one among many of the new synthetic abortifacients. But it has become a symbol of that development—and thus is very nearly sacrosanct.

Etienne-Emile Baulieu, the chief developer and crusading promoter of the drug, says with no little hyperbole that it is "the most important invention of the twentieth century," and that it therefore has been rightfully "elevated to mythic status."[6]

Apparently his assessment is something more than political posturing or personal braggadocio—for he is by no means alone.

According to Patricia Ireland, the president of the National Organization for Women (NOW), the drug is indeed "symbolic of the battle for women's rights. It is the cornerstone of our future."[7]

Molly Yard, who was Ireland's immediate predecessor at NOW, agrees saying that RU-486 is "a most critical drug"—perhaps even "the most significant medical advance in human history and the symbol of a brighter future for women everywhere."[8]

Paul Ehrlich, population researcher and author, asserts it is the "medical breakthrough" that "women everywhere have been hoping and praying for."[9]

Nita Lowey, a Congresswoman from New York, claims it is

"an important medical innovation that could dramatically enhance women's privacy and health."[10]

Eleanor Smeal, president of the Feminist Majority Foundation, says RU-486 is a "truly remarkable" drug that has "amazing properties which hold tremendous promise for the benefit of women." Indeed, she bubbles, it is "an historic breakthrough in medicine."[11]

Syndicated columnist and pro-abortion mouthpiece Ellen Goodman opined that "RU-486 offers the best possibility of muting the abortion conflict while at the same time protecting privacy." That is a marriage that she apparently believes was made in Heaven.[12]

But the most laudatory praise of all comes from Lawrence Lader, longtime abortion advocate and founder of the National Abortion Rights Action League. He said:

> RU-486 presents a classic case of how scientific progress can revolutionize our lives. Within the last century, the railroad opened up Western America and became a major factor in turning the United States into an economic colossus. The elevator was essential to the development of the skyscraper, the vertical city, and the concentration of business and services in a unified geographic area. The automobile gave us more than speed; it opened up the suburbs and the possibility of combining a rural or semi-rural lifestyle with employment in the central city. The cathode-ray tube made television possible. Antibiotics and other pioneering drugs extended our life-span and improved the quality of these added years. But when it comes to making an impact on our personal relationships, the science of controlling human reproduction must be considered unique. No other development—not even the telephone, with its advantage of bringing families and friends together—has so drastically changed our lives.[13]

According to Lader, "With the development of RU-486, scientific progress has reached a whole new stage."[14]

It is difficult to argue with an invention that is touted as even more significant than the railroad, the elevator, the automobile, television, antibiotics, and the telephone—one that would put an end to bitterness and strife and offer mankind a dazzling new hope.

But there are those who would argue with it anyway—difficult task or not. It seems that not everyone is enamored by the drug. In fact, many are downright hostile toward it. Internationally, virtually every pro-life organization has vociferously condemned RU-486. With a single voice they have signaled their opposition to its continued development and distribution.

Joseph Scheidler, director of the Pro-Life Action League and one of the patriarchs of the modern pro-life movement, says that the drug is little more than "a human pesticide." It is very simply "bad medicine," he says, and could eventually prove to be nothing less than a "prescription for disaster."[15]

Another of the pro-life movement's patriarchs, Paul Marx, has called RU-486 "chemical warfare on our families and a threat to the vitality of our civilization."[16]

Jack Willke, the longtime spokesman for the international Right to Life community, has labeled the drug as nothing less than a "chemical killer."[17]

Bernard Nathanson, a renowned former abortionist who supplies technical support to medical practitioners and ethicists, has said it is simply "the latest in a series of weapons in the burgeoning biological warfare against the unborn."[18]

William Brennan, a respected professor at St. Louis University, has gone even further:

Today's world of exterminative medicine is dominated by a relentless search for the quickest, safest, and most effective method of doing away with the unwanted unborn. In this fiercely competitive milieu of scientific barbarism, the field of chemistry continues to play a leading role. RU-486 is merely the latest chemical agent directed against the innocent.[19]

And so, at the second World Congress for Life in Tokyo in 1991, a resolution was overwhelmingly passed by the international delegates calling for the "immediate withdrawal of RU-486 from the market."[20] In addition, the attendees called for a comprehensive boycott of all Roussel-Uclaf and Hoechst affiliates and subsidiaries worldwide—since they manufacture and distribute the drug—until it is out of production altogether.

According to Baulieu, such opposition ought to be dismissed out of hand as a "morally scandalous and inexplicable religious intolerance."[21]

Lader argues that critics are simply "extremists" and "fundamentalists" who stoop to "threats," "intimidation," and "violence."[22] Presumably, just to be so labeled is enough to exclude them from any serious participation in the public debate.

Kate Michelman, the executive director of the National Abortion Rights Action League, concurred saying, "The uproar over RU-486 exposes the darkest, ugliest secret of the anti-choice movement: an unrelenting fanaticism coupled with an almost total disregard for the health and lives of women."[23]

And abortion entrepreneur Larry Ottenger opined that anyone who has the temerity to disparage the wonder drug must be a "schizophrenic crank bent on undoing the advances of modern medicine."[24]

There is no middle ground. Symbols never induce ambivalence—there are only iconoclasts[25] or iconodules.[26]

Why does this drug elicit such wildly varying responses and provoke such cantankerous name-calling? And how did it come to be the symbol of the abortion struggle?

A QUICK FIX

"If the medieval alchemists knew what we know today," says Ottenger, "they would have tried to turn baser elements into RU-486 instead of gold. It is that valuable. It is a mother lode of modern magic."[27]

"No way," counters Herna Hroz, a pro-life leader in Croatia. "If this drug is any kind of gold, it is fool's gold. If it is any kind of magic, it is black magic."[28]

Either way—whether it is actually of Midas or of Medusa—one thing is perfectly clear: RU-486, besides being a controversial political symbol, is a remarkable pharmaceutical development.

The drug—like so many of the new abortifacients—is a computer-designed synthetic steroid analog. An altered form of norethindrone—an artificial hormonal agent first used in the original birth control pill—it works to subvert the natural action of progesterone in the uterus.

Progesterone is a hormone that is naturally produced by a woman's body during the last two weeks of her regular menstrual cycle. It plays a central role in the establishment and maintenance of any possible pregnancy by creating an appropriately hospitable environment in the uterus. It is in fact the *sine qua non* of pregnancy.

Its operating mechanism is a marvel of God's complex creative design. Each month an egg develops in a follicle of the ovary. After ovulation is triggered by a surge of a luteinizing agent secreted by the pituitary gland, what is left of the ovarian follicle develops into something called the corpus luteum. This is what actually secretes the progesterone hormone.

At that point, the hormone begins to act on the endometrium of the uterus to prepare it for the implantation of a newly conceived embryo. If indeed conception has taken place, then the tiny child will enter the uterus from the fallopian tube and implant himself in the endometrium. The nascent placenta then begins discharging chorionic gonadotrophin, thus signaling the corpus luteum to continue production of progesterone. This will support the endometrium, relax any contractions in the uterine muscle, firm the cervix, and inhibit possible dilation. If conception has not occurred, then progesterone production gradually ceases and menstruation begins.

Etienne-Emile Baulieu—a maverick French researcher who began his medical career working on the first generation of birth control pills—convinced the pharmaceutical giant Roussel-Uclaf to allow him to pursue anti-progesterone tests with a cholesterol-derived steroid compound the company had recently isolated— dubbed RU-486 or Mifepristone. He and his research staff believed that if they could somehow obstruct or neutralize progesterone with such an anti-hormone, any newly conceived child would not be able to attach itself to the womb. It would thus die and then be washed out of the uterus in an artificially provoked menses—a quick fix. That, at least, was their theory.

The blocking action would occur, they felt, when RU-486 molecules began to bind to the receptors in the endometrium—thus leaving nothing for the progesterone to attach itself to. Without a sufficient supply of active progesterone, the lining of the uterus would literally disintegrate and be sloughed off. In addition, the anti-progesterone action of the drug would soften the cervix, induce uterine contractions, and stimulate dilation. All of these actions together, they believed, would make pregnancy termination perfunctory.

In the initial clinical tests however, pregnancies proved to be much more durable than expected. Despite the radical hormonal changes in a woman's body effected by the drug and the hostile aggravating agents it looses in her uterus, her womb is a naturally protective environment. All too often, the anti-progesterone drug merely damaged a woman's uterus or her developing child. Or it would effectively kill the child but was unable to expel him. In test after test women experienced prolonged bleeding and required either the administration of a labor-inducing drug or an abortifacient suction procedure to remove the dead child. The failure rate of the drug hovered between 15 and 50 percent.[29]

Eventually the researchers were forced to admit that the only way to reduce that unacceptable level of abortive failure was to combine the drug with prostaglandin—which would supplement and accelerate the pregnancy expulsion as both a labor inducer and a uterine stripper. This enabled them to achieve a success rate somewhere between 89 and 95 percent.[30]

More than a hundred thousand women have taken RU-486 in clinical tests and consumer applications, but there are still a number of mysteries surrounding the drug's action.[31] For instance, though it binds to uterine receptors with an affinity about three times as great as progesterone itself, the drug possesses a bulky dimethylaminophenyl group which appears to prevent the change in receptor conformation necessary for the activation of gene transcription.[32] In addition, there has been substantial evidence of blood insolubility, adrenal incompatibility, and hormonal dysynchrony.[33] Thus, both the specter of short-term ineffectiveness and of long-term complications continue to haunt the drug's advocates—it is not quite the quick fix that Baulieu and Roussel had hoped for.[34]

Even so, the drug has been thrust into the forefront of the battle over abortion. Why and how are perhaps as mysterious as the anti-progesterone mechanism itself.

THE LONG AND WINDING ROAD

The development, testing, refinement, and distribution of RU-486 has followed a long and tortured course. But it is a course that helps throw a much needed spotlight on the arcane passions that have turned the drug into a political icon.

- In 1962 Dr. Gregory Pincus, the developer of the original birth control pill, postulated that if an anti-progesterone could ever be developed, it could very likely be used as an implantation inhibitor.

- Eight years later his young associate, Etienne-Emile Baulieu, began government-funded progesterone receptor research at Bicetre Hospital in Paris.

- Shortly thereafter, a team of French researchers began to experiment with computer-designed steroid hormones in an attempt to synthesize an anti-cortisone compound under the direction of Georges Teutsch, a chemist, and Daniel Philibert, a physician and pharmacologist.

- The researchers at Roussel-Uclaf, the firm that sponsored the studies, first synthesized RU-486 in early 1980, immediately noticing unique properties that indicated both glucocorticoid inhibitors and progesterone antagonists.

- Baulieu, now a consultant to Roussel, was invited to track a parallel line of studies two months later.

- Baulieu announced the first successful human testing of the drug as an abortifacient in April 1982.

- Beginning early the next year, small-scale clinical trials were initiated under the auspices of the World Health Organization and the Population Council.

- The American government awarded three major grants for RU-486 clinical research through the National Institutes of Health in 1983.

- At about the same time, substantial funding from the Ford, Rockefeller, and Mellon Foundations, as well as strategic support from the Hect Fund, the Lasker Fund, and Planned Parenthood, allowed experiments to move ahead without delay.

- In October 1984 scientists from seven countries working on RU-486 research met at the Rockefeller Foundation's conference and study center in Bellagio, Italy, to exchange their findings.

- The proceedings of the Bellagio conference were published in the influential book *The Anti-Progestin Steroid RU-486 and Human Fertility Control*, edited by Baulieu and Rockefeller staffer Sheldon Segal.

- In 1985 research in Sweden indicated that the drug's abysmal failure rate of 15 to 50 percent could be reduced significantly with a supplemental dose of prostaglandin to induce uterine contractions.

- Simultaneous testing began in America at the University of Southern California under the auspices of the Population Council.

- Late in 1986 two important articles appeared lauding the effectiveness of the drug—in the *New England Journal of Medicine* and the *Contraceptive Technology Update*.

- That same year Roussel researchers admitted that regular use of RU-486 actually interferes with the delicate balance in a woman's regular hormonal cycle and thus could not be used as a contraceptive—it could only be prescribed for abortifacient procedures.

- Planned Parenthood and several other pro-abortion organizations used their considerable media clout to launch a massive promotional campaign extolling the virtues of the drug throughout 1987.

- Because of poor clinical effectiveness, the French Health Ministry denied approval of the drug during the first month of 1988.

- Immediately, Roussel refiled an application for approval to use the abortifacient drug—this time in conjunction with prostaglandin.

- The French government's Market Authorization Committee of the Ministry of Health approved the drug for consumer use on September 23, 1988.

- Three days later the Food and Drug Administration issued an "Import Bulletin" prohibiting consumer entry and use of the drug in the United States.

- Reaction to the drug was immediate. Pro-life organizations denounced its approval and launched various protests and boycotts against Roussel and its giant parent company, Hoechst.

- In response to the public outcry, Hoechst officials pressured Roussel to withdraw the abortifacient from the world market on October 26, 1988.

- Two days later the French Minister of Health, Claude Evin, ordered the company to reinstate production and distribution "in the interest of the public health," saying that RU-486 was "the moral property of women, not just the property of the drug company."

- In December the French government formally authorized procedures for the distribution of the drug—including a written warning about the many possible risks and complications to the women who take it.

- In the first month of 1989 Roussel began a nationwide giveaway promotion for the drug—distributing it to some twenty thousand women.

- At the same time, a Gallup Poll published in *Health Week* magazine revealed that some 62 percent of all Americans opposed the production and distribution of "drugs for the sole purpose of causing abortions."

- On January 15, 1990, Dr. Andre Delmas and Dr. Pierre de Vernejoul, the president of France's National Academy of Medicine and the chairman of the Therapeutic Pharmacology Commission respectively, launched the International Inquiry Commission on RU-486 in the face of growing evidence of serious risks and complications.

- Unable to ignore the evidence any longer, the French government's Pharmaceutic National Committee issued a requirement on April 3, 1990 that warning labels accompany all future shipments of the drug specifically describing all possible dangers.

- Backtracking still further, the French government ruled in January 1991 that Health Minister Claude Evin never had the legal authority to force Roussel into resuming distribution of the drug—and that his two-year-old order had actually never gone into effect.

- That same year the New Hampshire Senate passed a controversial resolution calling for their state to become a testing ground for the drug—despite the fact that at least twelve active testing permits had been granted by the FDA already.

- The first confirmed death connected with RU-486 was reported by the French Health Ministry on May 23, 1991.

- During that same week, Baulieu was in Canada to address the Canadian Abortion Rights Action League saying that the drug would soon be approved for second and third trimester abortions.

- Over the next several days, new reports of possible deaths, serious permanent disabilities, comas, and cardiac arrests began to surface regularly—but were downplayed by the media.

- On April 10, 1991, ignoring the growing concerns in the medical community, longtime abortion crusader Lawrence Lader launched a massive RU-486 promotional campaign and international book tour.

- The drug was approved for consumer use in Britain and three Scandinavian countries during that summer—with several other European Community nations indicating they would soon follow suit.

- In August Planned Parenthood revealed that it had hammered out an aggressive strategy with Roussel's president, Edouard Sakiz, to form a pharmaceutical company that would secure distribution rights for the drug in countries where there was "political or religious resistance."

- At an embarrassingly small counter-protest and rally in Wichita, Kansas—where tens of thousands of pro-life citizens had previously demonstrated their resolve to rid their city of an insidious abortuary that specialized in child-killing procedures well into the eighth and ninth months—several prominent feminist activists promised to make the battle over RU-486 the "most bitterly fought crusade in our nation's history."

Clearly the short but tumultuous history of RU-486 has been a long and winding road of setbacks, switchbacks, and comebacks. Such a record leaves a number of questions yet unanswered: Is it really safe? Is it really effective? Is it really easy? Is it really private? And is it really a breakthrough?

In short, is it a substantive advance in women's health care or just a *shibboleth* in the battle over abortion?

IS IT SAFE?

According to virtually all the pro-abortion pundits, RU-486 is entirely safe for the mother—with even fewer risks and complications than the widely used surgical procedures.[35] In fact, it is often praised as a great advancement in health care for women.[36]

"Extensive testing in Europe indicates that RU-486 is a safe, reliable, and relatively inexpensive alternative to surgical abortion," Kate Michelman says. "It may have the potential to save the lives of thousands of women."[37]

Ben Graber, an abortionist who also serves as a legislator in the state of Florida, asserted that the "promising" drug was "an excellent medication" and said he was certain it would prove to be "beneficial to lots of people."[38]

Ardent abortion supporter Allan Rosenfield, director of the School of Public Health at Columbia University, says that fears of risks and complications "are based on fiction."[39]

Patricia Ireland boasts that the effects of RU-486 are "no worse than those of surgical abortion and possibly better."[40]

According to developer Baulieu, the drug has proven itself to be "meticulously safe" with only a few occurrences of "minor side effects."[41]

But all that may be stretching things just a bit.

According to a special report in the *American Druggist*, those minor side effects can actually be quite "nasty."[42]

Indeed they can.

In a recent clinical study in Britain, five hundred eighty-eight women were given abortions with RU-486 combined with the prostaglandin gemeprost. Five of the women bled so much that they required transfusions. One hundred sixty-six of them needed narcotics to ease the pain. Some one hundred and fifty vomited, and another seventy-three suffered diarrhea. Thirty-five failed to abort and had to undergo a follow-up surgical procedure. And together they averaged more than twenty days of heavy bleeding afterwards.[43]

And that report is by no means an isolated anomaly. Again and again, wherever RU-486 has been tested, serious complications have been reported.

Early in 1990, an International Inquiry Commission on RU-486 was established in Puteaux, France, to investigate the wide range of these alleged medical hazards. Ten of the most highly regarded medical and pharmaceutical researchers in Europe—including the current presidents of the French National Academy of Medicine and the National Pharmacological Commission—examined every shred of clinical and consumer data on the drug. Their final report was more than a little disturbing. Besides the common side effects of nausea, diarrhea, and irregular pulse, they found that "abnormal uterine metrorrhagia"[44] developed "in more than ninety percent of the cases." Moreover, an average drop of 30 percent in haematocrite[45] was observed. "That may partially explain," they argued, "the unduly high incidence of coronarite crises."[46] Finally, they noted "a strong stimulating effect by RU-486 on the growth of a breast cancerous cellular line" and "notably severe inhibitory properties on the immunitory system."[47]

Shortly after the report was released, Roussel-Uclaf admitted that nearly 10 percent of all the women who had used the drug experienced "undesirable side effects." Two life-threatening heart attacks had been reported: one myocardial infarction and one cardiac arrest. In addition, they revealed that another woman had fallen into a coma for more than thirty-six hours following the administration of the procedure.

When the first RU-486-related deaths were reported in the spring of 1991, the French Ministry of Health—which had once heralded the drug as the "moral property" of women—instituted new regulations:

- The RU-486 and prostaglandin combination may not be given to women who smoke or have diabetes.
- It may not be given to women over thirty-five years of age.

- The abortionist must have immediate access to cardio-pulmonary resuscitation equipment.
- The average dosage of prostaglandin must be halved from 0.25 milligrams to 0.125 milligrams.[48]

When questioned about these precautions, Roussel-Uclaf's official spokeswoman, Catherine Euvrard, explained simply that the drug was "too dangerous" to remain in use with "unregulated abandon."[49]

"After twenty years of a women's health movement that was supposed to make us more critically aware," says Patricia Hynes, who runs the Institute on Women and Technology at MIT, "I'm astounded—given fiascoes such as DES—by the uncritical rush toward RU-486."[50]

Hynes recruited three medical experts to review all the extant literature on RU-486 abortions. Their one hundred page report raises a number of stupefying concerns ranging from next-birth deformities to cardio-pulmonary arrest. "RU-486 has a high failure rate on its own," says Lynette Dumble, director of transplantation research at the University of Melbourne in Australia and a coauthor of the report. "Then they use a prostaglandin that has bad side effects. So you end up with two bad chemicals and no long term follow-up." She concludes, "Why would you want to run with those odds?"[51]

Why indeed?

IS IT EFFECTIVE?

Virtually every major medical journal on the European continent, in Britain, and in America have praised the abortifacient effectiveness of RU-486—from *Lancet*[52] to *The New England Journal of Medicine*,[53] from *The British Medical Journal*[54] to *Fertil Steril*,[55] and from *The British Journal of Family Planning*[56] to *JAMA*.[57]

That is certainly a formidable array of defenders. But even the most cursory examination of those reports reveals a whole host of unanswered difficulties—the chief of which is that the drug simply doesn't work very well. How it can be dubbed "effective" with a stand-alone failure rate of between 15 and 50 percent is itself a marvel of modern medicine.[58]

Even with the addition of the prostaglandin, the failure rate is abysmally high. One out of every twenty RU-486 abortions fails—whereas only one in two hundred surgical suction procedures need to be repeated.[59]

That is why high-profile abortionists such as Philip Stubblefield have had the audacity to question the wisdom of staking the credibility of the pro-abortion movement on such shaky turf. He said RU-486 "probably represents a technical advance where none is needed, at least not very much"—especially given the fact that the drug is not particularly safe and not particularly effective.[60]

But there may be an even darker side to the specter of the drug's ineffectiveness. Besides doubling the risk of ordinary complications, French researchers have now admitted that when the administration of RU-486 and prostaglandin fail to cause a complete abortion, "the question arises whether the fetus is harmed if the pregnancy continues." Animal tests, they noted, have revealed that the drug causes "deformities in the skull of the fetus." And further, "prostaglandins have been reported to be teratogenic[61] in both animals and humans." Thus, developmental malformations are more than a little likely.[62]

In light of those revelations, Anna Desilets, executive director of Alliance for Life in Canada, asserted that "Women should question whether RU-486 is the DES or Thalidomide of the nineties."[63] After all, even the drug's champions admit that "the first generation of RU-486 users will be guinea pigs for the drug's long term side effects."[64]

IS IT EASY?

Ease is a major selling point for RU-486. No muss. No fuss. Just take a pill and problem pregnancies simply vanish.

According to David Andrews, who recently served a stint as the acting president of Planned Parenthood, with RU-486 "abortion becomes as easy as visiting a doctor for a prescription."[65]

And the medical director of Planned Parenthood of New England, Judith Tyson, says that the procedure is "so simple" that many women will take the drug "never knowing whether they were pregnant" in the first place. "This is a perfect solution. Basically it just eliminates the whole question, and I think it's very nice that way."[66]

But as it turns out, it is not quite that easy after all. Or nice.

Even the president of Roussel-Uclaf, Edouard Sakiz, admits that "as abortion procedures go RU-486 is not at all easy to use." He pointed out that "it is much more complex to use" than vacuum aspiration and requires more time because "the woman has to live with her abortion for at least a week with this technique." He confessed that "it's an appalling psychological ordeal."[67]

RU-486 abortions call for at least four separate visits to the doctor over a period of three weeks. On the first visit the patient receives a full physical examination—often including a vaginal sonogram to establish pregnancy. Since the procedure is only effective up to seven weeks following a missed menstrual period, precise timing is essential at this stage. After a week-long "reflection" period, the client visits a clinic where she swallows three RU-486 pills. Then, on the third visit—this time either to a hospital or an abortion clinic equipped with complete non-ambulatory facilities—she receives an intramuscular injection of a prostaglandin. She is monitored there for about three to four hours and treated for the most common side effects. Three out of four women abort their children there, while the remainder must go home and wait.

Finally, about a week later, the fourth visit confirms the death of the child and the recovery of the mother.[68]

Not only is the process long and protracted, it is physically painful and psychologically debilitating.[69] *Newsweek* regretfully but honestly reported, "RU-486 is not the miraculous, painless, private morning-after drug that some have envisioned."[70] That is the height of understatement.

IS IT PRIVATE?

Still another major selling-point for the drug is that it purports to lend women far more privacy in their reproductive health maintenance—as an at-home, do-it-yourself abortion technique.

Thus, according to Lawrence Lader:

> The crowning achievement of RU-486 is that it gives women the option of more privacy in their child-bearing decisions. Only the woman and her doctor need ever know that she has taken the pill, and followed it with an injection or a suppository a day or two later. Women do not need an institutional setting since they only experience bleeding similar if slightly heavier than their menstrual flow.[71]

"RU-486 could make surgical abortions obsolete" is the refrain heard again and again from the drug's advocates. According to Kate Michelman, "It could take reproductive decisions out of the political arena and put them back in the privacy of our homes."[72]

And Ellen Goodman asserted that the drug "would put most early abortions into a very private realm. A woman could get an abortion simply by swallowing."[73]

Once again though, RU-486 fails to live up to the claims of its partisans.

Because the medicinal abortion procedure is so complex and so dangerous, a woman must ford a veritable river of doctors, technicians, nurses, midwives, and administrators in order to submit herself to the three-week-long ordeal. Besides the four clinical visits, she must be psychologically screened and administratively approved. She has to sign waivers and releases. She must supply a family medical profile. And she must undergo post-procedural counseling.[74]

That is hardly the "non-invasive" and "non-intrusive" privacy panacea that the pro-abortion minions have promised.[75] In fact, it may very well "wrench women and families into a terrible display of the consequences of medical technology run amuck," says Joseph Scheidler, "where any notions of privacy will be dashed on the rocks of widespread public scrutiny."[76]

In the United States, the Food and Drug Administration imposed a consumer import ban on the drug in the fear that someone might actually believe the privacy rhetoric and poison themselves. Frank Young, the FDA commissioner, warned:

> The intended use of this drug makes it likely it would be used without the benefit of the supervision of a physician, and indiscriminate use could be hazardous to the patient's health because the drug has potential side effects such as uterine bleeding, severe nausea, vomiting, and weakness.[77]

In other words, both the drug and the arguments that surround it are prescriptions for disaster.

IS IT A BREAKTHROUGH?

According to the common wisdom, RU-486 is not just an abortifacient. It is instead a versatile medical miracle with more uses than Dr. Bronner's Peppermint Oil Soap.

Ellen Goodman exults:

> So far, RU-486 has been shown to be useful in easing labor and treating Cushings disease. It has shown promise for the treatment of ovarian and breast cancer, endometriosis, and even brain tumors.[78]

Another journalist gushed that it might prove to be effective against "infertility" and "obesity" as well.[79]

According to William Regelson, a cancer specialist at the Medical College of Virginia, "If RU-486 were not an abortifacient, it would be considered a major medical breakthrough." He criticizes pro-life forces for "keeping the drug out of the hands" of researchers. He says simply, "the politics of abortion are blocking this drug" and as a result "lives are at stake."[80]

It sounds almost too good to be true. And in fact it is.

Although limited testing has begun for a number of other applications for RU-486—with full FDA approval in the United States and under the auspices of the World Health Organization elsewhere—*its only proven use is as an abortifacient.*

That is the only reason that in America the FDA has issued import restrictions on the drug. Jeff Nesbit, a spokesman for the agency, said it fails to meet the three most basic criteria for importation:

> A personally imported drug must be aimed at a serious or life threatening illness, there has to be no existing standard therapy for the illness, and there have to be no safety questions.[81]

RU-486 fails on all counts. As Richard Glassow, a chemical abortifacient expert, argues:

Abortion pill supporters have exaggerated very small and pre-liminary research results into impressive sounding gains in areas of intense public interest, such as breast cancer and endometriosis. There is no scientific evidence showing that RU-486 has any proven use except to kill unborn babies.[82]

The initial report of the International Inquiry Commission on RU-486 concurred saying, "There is as of yet, absolutely no evi-dence that the compound has any therapeutic usefulness. Mere speculation is not enough to warrant the serious attention of the scientific community."[83]

Perhaps failing all else, advocates of the drug are simply indulging in a little wishful thinking. Or perhaps more than just a little.

THE MYTHOS

The evidence is indisputable. RU-486 doesn't work very well. It isn't very safe. It isn't very convenient. And it doesn't offer any significant advance over current child-killing procedures.

So why have pro-abortion forces rallied around it with such a passionate don't-confuse-me-with-the-facts commitment? Why would they deliberately tie this chemotherapeutic albatross to the neck of their movement? What sort of twisted sense does that make?

The answer is simply that the importance of RU-486 tran-scends the facts. It transcends intellectual integrity, technological practicality, and medical applicability. It has ascended into the rarefied air of mythic sanctity.

According to Marie Bass, "RU-486 has become a metaphor for the entire abortion debate." Bass, who runs a public relations and lobbying firm that specializes in pro-abortion activity, admits that the symbolic significance of the drug seems at first sight to be seriously overwrought. "I get uncomfortable sometimes that so much of the focus is on RU-486," she says. But because it has been enshrined in the unquestionable pantheon of the pro-abortion cultus, she confesses, "we really do not have any choice."[84]

Myths, according to theologian J. I. Packer, are "stories made up to sanctify social patterns."[85] They are little more than lies carefully designed to reinforce a particular philosophy or morality within a culture. They are symbolic instruments of manipulation and control.

When Jeroboam splintered the nation of Israel after the death of Solomon, he knew that in order to consolidate his rule over the northern faction he would have to wean the people from their spiritual and emotional dependence on the Temple in Jerusalem. So he manufactured a system of rituals, emblems, and myths. He instituted a symbolic feast, at a symbolic shrine, attended by symbolic priests, before symbolic gods. Jeroboam's mythology sanctified a whole new set of social patterns. What would have been unthinkable before—idolatry, apostasy, and travesty—became almost overnight not only thinkable or acceptable, but conventional and habitual. As a result, the new king was able to manipulate and control his subjects.

The powerful, the would-be-powerful, and the wish-they-were-powerful have always relied on such maneuvers. Plato and Thucydides observed this phenomenon during the golden era in Greece.[86] Plutarch and Augustine identified it during the long epoch of Roman glory.[87] Sergios Kasilov and Basil Argyros noted it during the Byzantine millennium.[88] Niccolo Machiavelli and Thomas More recognized its importance during the European renaissance.[89] And Aleksandr Solzhenitsyn and Colin Thubron have pointed it out in our own time.[90] None of those myth-makers actually believed in their gods upon Olympus, across the River Styx, or within the Kremlin Palace. But as high priests of manipulation and control, they used those symbols to dominate the hearts and minds and lives of the masses.

Such men are always full of deceitful words (Psalm 36:3). Their counsel is deceitful (Proverbs 12:5). Their favor is deceitful (Proverbs 27:6). And their hearts are deceitful (Mark 7:22). They defraud the unsuspecting (Romans 16:18), displaying the spirit of anti-Christ (2 John 7), all for the sake of wealth, prestige, and pre-rogative (Proverbs 21:6).

Such puissance is in the long run all too fleeting (Revelation 21:8), because myth-makers do not go unpunished (Proverbs 19:5). Ultimately their sin finds them out (Jeremiah 17:11). Even so, their lies continue to wreak havoc among the innocent (Micah 6:12).

The effectiveness and desirability of RU-486 is merely a myth designed to achieve certain social and political ends—and thus not only must we be alert to its deception (Ephesians 4:14), testing those deceptions against the standard of truth (1 John 4:1-6), but we must expose its deceptions as well (Ephesians 5:11).

> Woe to the bloody city, completely full of lies and pillage; her prey never departs. (Nahum 3:1)

3

The Holy Grail

Ab Aeterno[1]

*There are those who believe that a new modernity
demands a new morality. What they fail to consider is
the harsh reality that there is no such thing as a new
morality. There is only one morality. All else is
immorality. There is only true Christian ethics over
against which stands the whole of paganism. If we are
to fulfill our great destiny as a people, then we must
return to the old morality, the sole morality.*[2]

THEODORE ROOSEVELT

*Nonsense is nonsense whether it rhymes or not, just as
bad half-pennies are good for nothing whether they
jingle or lie quiet.*[3]

CHARLES H. SPURGEON

IN the prosaic blue-collar English neighborhood where Clara
Darman grew up, resentment was as common as hedgerows.
She was a part of that spoiled post-war generation that was
rudely awakened to the fact they might never be able to attain to

the prosperity of their parents—at least not without paying the grueling price their parents had.

Their tightly packed row-houses and tiny hip-pocket gardens became emblematic for them of a society where no one is ever alone but is always lonely nonetheless. As prosperity passed them by, they gradually came to believe that the vehicle of their civilization was merely the luxurious giant whim of powerful malefactors, that the narrow suburban streets they had played on as children were paved with the gold of avarice, and that the traffic there was fitfully directed by robber barons.

By the time she enrolled at the University of East Sussex, Clara was already well-versed in the rhetoric of rancor and envy—she had become a thoroughly modern and liberated woman. She wore all the right clothes—dark and dismal. She listened to all the right music—angry and discordant. She went to all the right meetings—strident and bombastic. And she believed all the right things—nihilistic and *angst*-ridden.

She was a picture of insolence.

She committed her weekends at home in Brighton to "evangelizing" at the Royal Pavilion and Churchill Square with a grubby little stack of out-of-date issues of *Marxism Today*. She regularly worked herself into a piqued frenzy over such things as chlorofluorocarbons, plastic milk cartons, and styrofoam McDonalds packages. She waxed eloquent about *apartheid* in South Africa, deforestation in Brazil, whale harvesting in Japan, acid rain in Canada, and the international conspiracy of the Elders of Zion. She was heartbroken over what she was sure was the fraudulent electoral rejection of Daniel Ortega in Nicaragua. She was dumbfounded by the collapse of the worker's paradise in Eastern Europe. And she was flabbergasted by the de-sovietization of Gorbachev's *perestroika*.

Early on, Clara had become lemming-like in her hipper-than-thou, perennially-indignant, and compulsively-correct political associations. She joined Greenpeace, of course. And Amnesty International. But she also became a member of the Committee in Solidarity with the People of El Salvador, Housing Now, People for the Ethical Treatment of Animals, the African National Congress, the Sierra Club, and the New Internationalist Women's Cooperative. She even bathed with Body Shop soaps, ate Ben and Jerry's ice cream, and wore Birkenstock knock-offs and a cheap dangling nose-ring.

Like any good atheist, she knew what she knew. But like any good agnostic, she did not know what she did not know.

When she became pregnant during her sophomore year, Clara did exactly what was expected of her—she scheduled an appointment for an abortion at a local public health center. But several of her friends convinced her that a surgical abortion was passé. RU-486 was in fashion, and they persuaded her to investigate it.

After a prolonged ordeal, Clara was able to undergo the procedure. It was supposed to put an end to her worries. But it was only just the beginning of them.

"From what I have now come to understand," she told me, "I really had an easy time of it—at least compared with others who have taken the drug. I didn't have any life-threatening complications or anything like that. But I sure was miserable. I went into the clinic all cocky and self-assured. But after almost a week of violent cramps, nausea, and diarrhea, I wasn't so confident. And the incessant bleeding worried me."

The doctors informed her she was going to be just fine—everything was perfectly normal. But she wasn't so sure.

"The bleeding wouldn't stop," she said. "After two weeks I began to get really worried. Again though, the clinic told me just to relax—that kind of reaction to the treatment was not at all out of the ordinary, they said. Still, I couldn't help but believe anything that disruptive and distressing had to be bad for me."

But the physical side effects were the least of Clara's worries.

"My conscience was awakened like never before. I started thinking about what I had done. I was guilty and I felt it—and the physical trauma I was going through only heightened that kind of brooding. I couldn't escape the certain knowledge that I had been living a lie for far too long. And that now I had inflicted the consequences of my own dishonesty on an innocent child—my own child."

When she tried to explain her feelings to her friends, they gaped at her resentfully—with looks that would fell birds.

"They were completely blind to what I was going through. Somehow they thought my abortion should be a badge of honor— a kind of sacramental epiphany. They seemed to actually revel in it. They approached the whole subject with a religious carnival spirit. It was almost as if they had just vicariously participated in some long-anticipated arcane ritual. They mocked my squeamishness and derided my reticence. I felt grief-stricken and ashamed. But I also felt disoriented, lost, and alone. As they chattered gleefully, it began to dawn on me that I really didn't know them at all—and they really didn't know me. Our relationships had been built on shallow fads and fancies that had no relevance to the real world whatsoever. I couldn't decide who was the bigger fool, them or me."

It was suddenly obvious to her that to have a horror of the bourgeois is frightfully bourgeois, that nonconformity is always terrible in its avid conformity, and that despoiling life to the uttermost necessarily means begetting death to the outermost. She discovered that radicalism, like most other ancient religions, is largely made up of false prophesies and unshackled perversities.

"I looked at my friends, and shivers went up and down my spine. I understood for the first time the implications of our beliefs

and actions. I realized that death was not just an unhappy consequence of our philosophy—it was actually barbarically essential to
it. It always had been—and it always would be."

ANCIENT ARTS

According to G. K. Chesterton, throughout human history "there
is above all, this supreme stamp of the barbarian; the sacrifice of
the permanent to the temporary."[4]

Indeed, since the dawning of recorded history man has always
had a suppressed fascination with death. Like a moth drawn to a
candle flame, it seems that man compulsively deals in death—for
that is his nature (Romans 5:12).

At the time of the primordial Garden Fall, man was suddenly
bound into a covenant with death (Isaiah 28:15). Whether consciously or not, man became morbidly consumed with death
(Jeremiah 8:3). Though carefully camouflaged by polite social con-
vention, it became his basest motivation and incentive (Psalm
49:14). His mind became obsessed with it (Romans 8:6), his heart
was fixed on it (Proverbs 21:6), and his flesh was ruled by it
(Romans 8:2). "There is a way that seems right to a man, but its
end is the way of death" (Proverbs 14:12; 16:25).

The fact is, all men have fallen irrevocably into the grip of sin
(Romans 3:23). And "the wages of sin is death" (Romans 6:23).

It is no wonder, then, that brutal forms of abortion and infanticide have always been normal—though admittedly, distasteful—
aspects of human relations. Men have always contrived ingenious
diversions to satisfy their fallen passions. And child-killing has
invariably been noticeably prominent among them.

Virtually every culture in pagan antiquity pursued the ribald
saturnalia death dream of separating sex from responsibility—and
was thus stained with the blood of innocent children:

- Unwanted infants in ancient Rome were abandoned outside the city walls to die from exposure to the elements or from the attacks of wild foraging beasts.

- Greeks often gave their pregnant women harsh doses of herbal or medicinal abortifacients.

- Persians developed highly sophisticated surgical curette procedures.

- Chinese women tied heavy ropes around their waists so excruciatingly tight that they either aborted or passed into unconsciousness.

- Ancient Hindus and Arabs concocted chemical pessaries—abortifacients that were pushed or pumped directly into the womb through the birth canal.

- Primitive Canaanites threw their children onto great flaming pyres as a sacrifice to their god Molech.

- Polynesians subjected their pregnant women to onerous tortures—beating their abdomens with large stones or heaping hot coals upon their bodies.

- Japanese women straddled boiling caldrons of parricidal brews.

- Egyptians disposed of their unwanted children by disemboweling and dismembering them shortly after birth. Their collagen was then ritually harvested for the manufacture of cosmetic creams.

It is distressing to find that none of the great minds of the ancient world—from Plato and Aristotle to Seneca and Quintilian, from Pythagoras and Aristophanes to Livy and Cicero, from Herodotus and Thucydides to Plutarch and Euripides—discouraged or disparaged child-killing in any way. In fact, most of them quietly recommended it.

Man perennially tosses lives like dice—for both pleasure and profit.

Abortion and infanticide were so much a part of human societies, they even figured prominently in folklore and literature—providing a dominant literary *leitmotif* in those societies' traditions, stories, myths, fables, and legends. For example:

- The founding of Rome was, according to popular mythology, the happy result of the failed infanticide of two newborns, Romulus and Remus.

- Oedipus was also presumed to be an abandoned child who was mercifully rescued by a lowly shepherd.

- Ion was a celebrated monarch in ancient Greece who, according to tradition, miraculously lived through a brutal abortion procedure.

- Cyrus, the founder of the Persian empire, was supposedly a fortunate survivor of infanticide.

- According to Homer's legend, Paris was also once the victim of abandonment—long before his amorous indiscretions started the Trojan War.

- According to the various folk tales about their lives, Telephus, the king of Mysia in Greece, and Habius, ruler of the Cunetes in Spain, had both been exposed as children.

- Zeus, chief god of the Olympian pantheon, himself had been abandoned as a child. And he in turn exposed his twin sons, Zethus and Amphion.

- Similarly, other myths related the fact that Poseidon, Aesculapius, Hephaistos, Attis, and Cybele had all been abandoned to die.

A CLASH OF CULTURES

Clearly abortion was woven into the very fabric of pagan cultures. It was almost second nature for the men and women of antiquity to kill their children. They saw nothing particularly cruel about it.

In fact, it was instinctive for them to seek new and more efficient methods of despoiling the fruit of their wombs. They believed it was completely justifiable.

Even so, it remained for the most part a very discreet affair. And it was almost always cloaked in regret. Shame and guile have from the beginning been unlikely private partners in the brash public enterprise of smiting God's image (Romans 1:18-32).

Throughout history, knowledge of abortifacient potions, elixirs, rituals, and procedures was entrusted to a small disreputable underground—mendicants, herbalists, alchemists, conjurers, sorcerers, soothsayers, or cabalists. Even in the most unabashedly and brutally perverse cultures, estimable citizens tried to keep a goodly distance between themselves and this distasteful business. Child-killing was merely tolerated as a necessary evil. But even that discomfiting compromise was challenged before long.

When successive waves of Christian missionaries first penetrated and finally converted those cultures, practicing abortionists were driven further and further from sight.[5] With one voice those Christian pioneers cried out across the gulf of time the Good News of love's transcendence and life's sanctity. They unanimously proclaimed the gospel—the victory of Christ Jesus over sin and death. And at great risk they authenticated that cry in the way they lived their lives. They demonstrated the proclamation in their actions— rescuing the innocent, the helpless, and the perishing at every opportunity, by every means.

In fact, any list of the heroes of the Church reads like a pro-life honor roll—from Athanasius to Augustine, from Polycarp to Patrick, from John Chrysostom to Amy Carmichael, from Francis of Assisi to Francis Schaeffer, and from Brother Andrew to Mother Theresa. Christians have always affirmed a single-minded and unerring front against the abomination of abortion.

The worldview of those Christians made their pro-life witness an inescapable consequence of faith.

According to the Bible, death is "the enemy" (1 Corinthians 15:26). Barrenness is "the curse" (Genesis 3:17-19). Both entered God's world of life and fruitfulness through sin (Romans 5:12). At the Fall, mankind was suddenly destined for death (Jeremiah 15:2). But the Lord God—the giver of life (Acts 17:25), the fountain of life (Psalm 36:9), the defender of life (Psalm 27:1), the prince of life (Acts 3:15), and the restorer of life (Ruth 4:15)—did not leave matters at that. He not only sent the message of life (Acts 5:20) and the words of life (John 6:68), He sent the light of life (John 8:12). He sent Christ, His only begotten Son—the life of the world (John 6:51)—to break the bonds of death (1 Corinthians 15:54-56). Jesus "tasted death for everyone" (Hebrews 2:9), actually "abolishing death" for the sake of all men (2 Timothy 1:10) and offering them new life (John 5:21).

As a result of the propagation of this worldview, the tolerable evil gradually became intolerable. Laws were passed. Penalties were exacted. And abortion almost became extinct altogether.[6]

Almost, but not quite.

The seeds of death continued to germinate in the rotting soil of sin—waiting for another day.

THE MIRROR OF MODERNITY

Faith Popcorn—no kidding, that is actually the name of one of the brightest marketing consultants working with Fortune 500 companies on Madison Avenue today—has said that "The future bears a great resemblance to the past, only more so."[7] The epoch of modernity—from the Victorian age to the present—has borne out the truth of that paradox.

Until the writings of Thomas Malthus made birth control a

matter of social urgency during the nineteenth century, the quest for effective contraceptives and abortifacients was a selfish, silent indulgence. It remained man's dirty little secret—driven underground by Christian consensus.

But with Malthus that changed—almost overnight.

He was an errant clergyman and an eccentric professor of political economy whose mathematical theories convinced an entire generation of scientists, intellectuals, and social reformers that the world was facing an imminent economic crisis caused by unchecked human fertility. According to his calculations, population naturally increases by a geometric ratio, while the means of subsistence only increases by an arithmetic ratio. Thus poverty, deprivation, and hunger are inevitable unless population can somehow be artificially restrained. Any responsible social policy must therefore impose population controls as the most pressing priority. In fact, Malthus argued, to attempt to deal with endemic needs in any other way could actually only aggravate the crisis all the more. As far as he was concerned, the very survival of the race depended on an immediate interference in the mechanisms of both the state and the family. The Christian consensus that had reshaped Western culture had to be rolled back to the old pagan ideals of yesteryear.

Malthus recommended that a kind of benevolent totalitarianism be imposed for the good of mankind. In his *magnum opus, An Essay on the Principle of Population*, he described his dystopic agenda:

> All children born, beyond what would be required to keep up the population to a desired level, must necessarily perish, unless room is made for them by the deaths of grown persons. Therefore we should facilitate, instead of foolishly and vainly endeavoring to impede, the operations of nature in producing this mortality; and if we dread the too frequent visitation of the horrid form of famine, we should sedulously encourage the

other forms of destruction, which we compel nature to use. Instead of recommending cleanliness to the poor, we should encourage contrary habits. In our towns, we should make the streets narrower, crowd more people into the houses, and court the return of the plague. In the country, we should build our villages near stagnant pools, and particularly encourage settlement in all marshy and unwholesome situations. But above all, we should reprobate specific remedies for ravaging diseases; and restrain those benevolent, but much mistaken men, who have thought they were doing a service to mankind by projecting schemes for the total extirpation of particular disorders.[8]

Malthus believed that if *man* was to survive, *men* would have to be sacrificed. For the the sake of the greater good, lesser evils would have to be embraced. Ultimately the materially poor, the spiritually diseased, the racially inferior, and the mentally incompetent would have to be eliminated. The only question was, how?

A few of the disciples of Malthus believed the solution to that dilemma was political—to restrict immigration, centralize planning, reform social welfare, and tighten citizenship requirements. Some others thought the solution was technological—to control agricultural production, regulate medical proficiency, and nationalize industrial efficiency.

But the vast majority of Malthusians felt the solution was genetic—to inhibit "bad racial stocks," discourage charity and benevolence, and "aid the evolutionary ascent of man." Through selective breeding, eugenic repatterning[9] and craniometric specificity,[10] they hoped to purify the bloodlines and improve the chromosomal stock of the "highest" and the "most fit"—i.e., Aryan—race. Through segregation, sterilization, birth control, and abortion, they hoped to winnow the "lower" and "inferior" races out of the population—like chaff from wheat.

These dystopic principles ultimately found their way into some of the most significant political and social programs of the last two centuries:

- Mary Wollstonecraft, a contemporary of Malthus, was the pioneer of the modern feminist movement. In *A Vindication of the Rights of Women*, she laid the ideological foundation that the next several generations of feminists—including Olive Schreiner, Anna Howard Shaw, Charlotte Perkins Gilman, Ellen Key, Ida Husted Harper, Harriot Stanton Blatch, Helen Gardener, Eliza Duffey, Frances Willard, and Emma Goldman—would ultimately build upon.[11] According to Goldman, that foundation necessitated clear-cut Malthusian ideals—the "elimination of the unfit" for the "ultimate good," the "perfection of the race," as well as the "shunting of archaic Christian ethical restrictions" that might "hinder a return to the saner societal norm of Greece and Rome."[12]

- Charles Darwin took the thinking of Malthus one step further. Postulating a worldview based on survival of the fittest, he had little sympathy for those species that seemed to be at the bottom of the evolutionary chain. His faithful disciples—who shaped the dogmas and the practical agendas of Social Darwinism—turned that lack of mercy into a veritable triage barrage. Michael Fletcher, a leading academic in the movement, asserted that "the task of all responsible men" was to "gently assist the forward progress of the evolutionary ascent" in both "positive and negative regards." The only real obstacle to this, he argued, was the "mindless interference of Christian bleeding-hearts" who would "sustain the weak and inferior races" longer than "their natural due."[13]

- Adolf Hitler adopted the ideas of Malthus in a wholesale fashion in his administration of the Third Reich. His exterminative "final solution," his coercive abortion program in Poland,

Yugoslavia, and Czechoslovakia, and his elitist national social-
ism all echoed the Malthusian call to "rid the earth of dysgenic
peoples by whatever means available" so that the elite might
"enjoy the prosperity of the Fatherland."[14] He also reiterated the
Malthusian ideal of eliminating any Christian mercy ministries
or social service programs. "Let us spend our efforts and our
resources," he implored, "on the productive, not on the
wastrel."[15]

- Josef Stalin also wove the Malthusian ideal into his brutal interpretation of Marxism. His terrible Ukrainian triage, his collectivization of the Kulaks, and his Siberian genocide were all
undertaken "for the good of the proletariat." He argued that
"The greatest obstacle to the successful completion of the people's revolution is the swarming of inferior races from the south
and east."[16] And the only thing that kept him from eliminating
that obstacle, he believed, was "the foolhardy interference of
church charity."[17] That is why he ultimately made all Christian
philanthropies illegal.

- Similarly, Margaret Sanger made Malthusian thinking the cornerstone of her endeavors. She was thoroughly convinced that
the "inferior races" were actually "human weeds" and a "men-
ace to civilization."[18] She believed "social regeneration" would
only be possible as the "sinister forces of the hordes of irre-
sponsibility and imbecility" were repulsed.[19] She accepted the
Malthusian notion that organized Christian charity to ethnic
minorities and the poor was a "symptom of a malignant social
disease" because it encouraged the prolificacy of "defectives,
delinquents, and dependents."[20] Those Malthusian notions were
then woven into the very fabric of the organization she founded
and led for nearly half a century—Planned Parenthood.[21]

Clearly, the practical import of Malthusianism—whether
grafted into Wollstonecraft's feminism, Darwin's evolutionism,

Hitler's Nazism, Stalin's communism, or Sanger's eugenicism—was that abortion and infanticide were advocated as social *virtues* and that traditional Christian values were derided as *vices*. Killing was offered as a beneficent solution to a plethora of planetary crises of monumental proportions. For almost the first time in history, a consistent pagan philosophy had been formulated not just to ethically defend genocide but to raise it to a new level of righteousness. Whereas most pagan societies of the past endorsed it as a distasteful but necessary aspect of the natural order, with Malthusianism death had been made "altruistic"—and a new movement was thus ensconced on the world's stage.

LOVE POTION NUMBER NINE

Political theorist Ayn Rand may well have had this chilling legacy of Malthus in mind when she said:

> Every major horror of history has been committed in the name of an altruistic motive. Has any act of selfishness ever equalled the carnage perpetrated by the disciples of altruism? Hardly.[22]

With the demise of ideological totalitarianism toward the end of the twentieth century, most Malthusians turned to the practical totalitarianism of social control through birth control as the last best hope of their "altruism." Undoubtedly it has become—as Margaret Sanger predicted it would—their "Love Potion" and their "Holy Grail."[23]

Interestingly, for them birth control has never meant contraception per se. Instead, it has meant anything that could guarantee the absolute separation of sex and procreation—and that ultimately has required at least a fall-back dependence on various forms of abortion. The reason is simple: no contraceptive technique is absolutely foolproof.

In the United States alone, 90 percent of the fifty-five million women of reproductive age who are "at risk" of unwanted pregnancies use some form of contraception,[24] including as many as 79 percent of all sexually active teens.[25] Even so, there are more than three million unwanted pregnancies reported annually.[26] There are more than fourteen million cases of venereal disease reported every year.[27]

The annual in-use failure rate for the pill is as high as 11 percent.[28] For the diaphragm, the normal failure rate is nearly 32 percent.[29] For the inter-uterine coil—or the IUD, as it is most often called—it is almost 11 percent.[30] For "safe sex" condoms, it is over 18 percent.[31] And for the various foam, cream, and jelly spermicides, it can range as high as 34 percent.[32] That means that a sexually active fourteen-year-old girl who faithfully uses the pill has a 44 percent chance of getting pregnant at least once before she finishes high school.[33] She has a 69 percent chance of getting pregnant at least once before she finishes college.[34] And she has a 30 percent chance of getting pregnant two or more times.[35] If she relies on "safe sex" condoms, the likelihood of an unwanted pregnancy while she is in school rises to nearly 87 percent.[36]

In other words, reliance on contraception virtually guarantees that women will get pregnant—and that they will then be forced to fall back on the birth control linchpin—abortion.

Birth control advocates know that only too well.

That is why virtually all the new drugs marshaled into the birth control arsenal have abortifacient actions—from Norplant and the Melatonin pill to Levonorgestrel coils and Capronor implants, from the low-level Estrogen pill and RU-486 to vaginal rings and transdermal patches.

And that is why abortion is such a big business. Abortion is the inescapable bottom line for the Malthusian "altruists."

Since its decriminalization some two decades ago, abortion has grown into a five hundred million dollar a year industry in America,[37] another half a billion dollars in Europe,[38] and an estimated ten billion dollars a year worldwide.[39] More than one hundred and twenty thousand women each day, almost forty-four million per year, resort to abortion and then to its various birth control subsidiaries.[40] It has thus become the most frequently performed surgical operation.[41] Undoubtedly, the mind-numbing vastness of this market has created unprecedented opportunities for a wildly profitable stock-in-trade.

The rush to get RU-486 to market is the direct result of those pressing opportunities—drawing two of the most significant instruments of Malthusian "altruism" into the medico-political limelight: Planned Parenthood and the Rockefeller Foundation.

PLANNED PARENTHOOD

Planned Parenthood is the world's oldest, largest, and best-organized provider of abortion and birth control services.[42] From its modest beginnings around the turn of the century, when the entire makeshift operation consisted of nothing more than a two-room makeshift clinic in a seedy Brooklyn neighborhood[43] staffed by three untrained volunteers,[44] it has expanded dramatically into a multibillion dollar international conglomerate with programs and activities in one hundred and twenty nations—on every continent.[45] In the United States—where the organization enjoys its strongest institutional support—it employs more than twenty thousand staff personnel and volunteers[46] in over eight hundred clinics,[47] nearly two hundred affiliates,[48] and more than fifty chapters[49] in every major metropolitan area coast to coast.[50]

In 1922 Margaret Sanger, Planned Parenthood's now-sainted founder, chided social workers, philanthropists, and churchmen for perpetuating "the cruelty of charity."[51] She argued that organized

attempts to help the poor were the "surest sign that our civilization has bred, is breeding, and is perpetuating constantly increas-
ing numbers of defectives, delinquents, and dependents."[52] She
went on to say that the most "insidiously injurious philanthropy"
was the maternity care given to poor women.[53] She concluded her
diatribe by describing all those who refused to see the necessity of
severely regulating the fertility of the working class as "benign
imbeciles, who encourage the defective and diseased elements
of humanity in their reckless and irresponsible swarming and
spawning."[54]

Her alternative to charity was "to eliminate the stocks" she felt
were most detrimental "to the future of the race and the world."[55]
To that end, Planned Parenthood has always targeted minorities,
the unwanted, and the disadvantaged for family limitation, abortion, and sterilization.[56] "More children from the fit, less from the
unfit," Sanger opined, "that is the chief issue of birth control."[57]
Showing her altruistic stripes, she said, "The most merciful thing
that a large family can do to one of its infant members is to kill
it."[58]

Thus, while the organization has often trumpeted its concerns about contraception, education, and maternal health, its
chief concern has always been to charitably eliminate the
unwanted. Animosity toward the weak and lowly has been its
hallmark from its earliest days.[59] In fact, its entire program of
family limitation was designed to foster an elitist decimation of
the underclasses.[60]

To this day Planned Parenthood's literature focuses on the "terrible burden" the poor place on the rich.[61] It is constantly remind-
ing us of the costs welfare mothers incur for the elite.[62] It is forever
devising new plans to penetrate black, Hispanic, and Third-World
communities with its crippling message of eugenic racism.[63] Its only
use for the deprived and rejected is as bait for huge federal subsi-

dies and foundation grants and as fodder for its lucrative abortion business. "If we must have welfare," Sanger argued, "give it to the rich, not to the poor."[64] For years, her organization has attempted to translate that philosophy into public policy.

Among the recently proposed measures Planned Parenthood has spotlighted in its literature are such things as the elimination of child care, medical attention, scholarships, housing, loans, and subsidies to poor families.[65] In addition, it has given voice to the suggestion that maternity benefits be drastically reduced or even eliminated, that substantial across-the-board marriage and child taxes be imposed, and that large families not be given preferential charitable relief.[66]

Utilizing its considerable wealth, manpower, and influence, Planned Parenthood has muscled its way into virtually every facet of modern life. It now plays a strategic role in the health and social services community.[67] It is actively involved in both advertising and programming in the mass media.[68] It exerts a major influence on public and private education.[69] It carries considerable political clout through lobbying, legislation, advocacy, campaigning, and litigation.[70] It is involved in publishing,[71] research,[72] medical technology,[73] judicial activism,[74] public relations,[75] foreign affairs,[76] psychological counseling,[77] sociological planning,[78] demographic investigation,[79] curriculum development,[80] pharmacological distribution,[81] theological reorientation,[82] and public legal service provision.[83]

When Planned Parenthood announced it was going to reinforce "its strategic investment in the development and distribution of RU-486" with "even more resources than ever before," it was signaling world opinion-makers that it really meant business—in more ways than one. Pledging to lay "whatever political, commercial, educational, medical, and pharmaceutical foundations may be necessary," the organization was throwing its full weight into the battle over the drug.[84]

And that is a lot of weight.

THE ROCKEFELLER FOUNDATION

When he first went into business, immediately after graduating from high school in 1855, John D. Rockefeller began his lifelong practice of tithing. As a deacon and Sunday school teacher at the Erie Street Baptist Church, he was absolutely ardent about the necessity for Christians to exercise wise stewardship over all God had entrusted to them. In 1858 he entered into commodities commission partnership in his hometown of Cleveland, Ohio. By 1863 the business had become prosperous enough to expand into the newly emerging oil industry. And by 1865 Rockefeller was able to buy his partners out, launching what would prove to be the most remarkable success story in American business history. Through it all he continued to give 10 percent of his vastly expanding wealth to his church and its various missionary endeavors. By the last decade of the nineteenth century, that amounted to well over a million dollars a year—an unfathomably huge sum in that day. But his commitment was unshakable. He said:

> God gave me my money. I believe that the power to make money is a gift to be developed and used to the best of our ability for the good of mankind. Having been endowed with the gift I possess, I believe it is my duty to make money and still more money and use the money I make for the good of my fellow man according to the dictates of my conscience.[85]

And his conscience dictated that he pour his charitable dollars primarily into church work—planting new Baptist missions, establishing new pastoral training centers, endowing universities, and supporting hospitals. He gave millions to the University of Chicago, for instance—which was a Baptist school begun by Stephen Douglas in 1856 as the Morgan Park Theological Seminary. Rockefeller also launched the Pioneer Baptist Church Establishment Agency and the Baptist Central Missionary Society as conduits for his ever-enlarging giving program.

By 1891, however, he discovered that finding worthy beneficiaries for his gifts was consuming nearly as much of his time as his business. Part of the problem was simply the immensity of the task. But worse than that were the dunning pleas from a myriad of grant-seekers. "Neither in the privacy of his home, nor at the table, nor in the aisles of his church, nor during business hours, nor anywhere else was he secure from insistent appeal," said Frederick T. Gates, a Baptist preacher Rockefeller often turned to for wise counsel. "He was constantly hunted, stalked, and hounded almost like a wild animal."[86]

Exhausted and frustrated, Rockefeller asked Gates to become his "chief almoner."[87] The minister immediately demonstrated unswerving discernment and a keen sense of business propriety. He began to evaluate every request for funds, draw up recommendations and guidelines for giving, and then follow up each gift to make certain it was spent responsibly.

Although the sums dispensed were quite sizable for the day, this was still quite a humble beginning for what would one day be a veritable philanthropic industry—one that would make the Rockefeller family an international institution. In 1913, after devising an entirely new legal trust structure—as revolutionary in its conception as the interstate industrial corporation had been two decades earlier—Gates and Rockefeller established the Rockefeller Foundation. It quickly became the most powerful and influential charitable organization in history.

Although it continued to place a heavy emphasis on Baptist

missions, the Foundation began a new series of ambitious projects that would literally help to reshape civilization.

- The Rockefeller Institute for Medical Research was launched— with an endowment of more than a million dollars to build and equip the finest laboratory in the world. Within a decade scientists there had developed treatments—or in some instances cures—for meningitis, yellow fever, infantile paralysis, and pneumonia.[88]

- The General Education Board was incorporated with more than ten million dollars. Beginning in the American South and West, it dramatically raised educational standards for the poor, for minorities, and for rural children, helping to establish more than eight thousand schools in less than five years.[89]

- The Rockefeller Sanitation Commission was established because the government of the United States simply did not have the resources to mount a serious campaign to rid the deep South of the blight of hookworm—but John D. Rockefeller did. The campaign was supremely successful, and great advances in public health care were made as a result.[90]

At the time of his death in 1937, Rockefeller had given away untold millions of dollars to innumerable worthy charities, ministries, and projects. But the most significant legacy of his wealth was yet to come. Under the leadership of his son and his grandsons, both the Foundation's endowment and reputation grew to spectacular proportions. And its projects were widely varying: from reconstructing colonial Williamsburg and preserving the Jackson Hole Conservation Area to establishing the Trilateral Commission and promoting the Council on Foreign Relations.[91]

Although the Foundation continued to set aside a huge proportion of its assets for religious charities, it funded fewer and fewer evangelistic or missionary endeavors. The sole but notable exceptions to this trend were its strong demonstrations of support for Billy Sunday and, much later, Billy Graham. Instead, it increasingly lent its resources to the emerging liberal religious establishment.

- It almost single-handedly established the interdenominational Riverside Church in New York City—an infamous bastion of Protestant radicalism—as a pulpit platform for Harry Emerson Fosdick following his celebrated heresy trial.[92]

- It launched the ill-fated Inter-Church World Movement—a precursor to the World Council of Churches.[93]

- It founded and endowed the renowned Union Theological Seminary and the Institute of Religious Research.[94]

- It funded an international assault on pornography and prostitution through its Bureau of Social Hygiene.[95]

- And it established the National Council of Churches to unify and coordinate all these efforts into a singular movement with a singular vision—a spiritual center for a "New World Order."[96]

One of the results of this new emphasis on liberal and international causes was that both the Rockefeller family and the Foundation were drawn into increasingly radical circles. Margaret Sanger, for instance, was able to influence several family members to lend their support to her eugenic schemes. Ever since, millions of Rockefeller dollars have poured into abortifacient research and development. In fact, through the years the Foundation provided a significant proportion of the funding for such groups as Princeton's Office of Population Research, Zero Population Growth, the Alan Guttmacher Institute, and Planned Parenthood while it single-handedly established the Population Council.

When Etienne-Emile Baulieu began looking for financial support for his RU-486 research, he had to look no further than the Rockefeller locus. According to Claude Foucault, a public relations specialist tapped by the French government to attract venture capital for the development of their drug, "The Rockefellers have an almost mystical power in the philanthropic world, so naturally I wanted to approach them first." He went on to say:

> Although they apparently have funded a number of bizarre fundamentalist kinds of things in the past, I found them all to be quite progressive. Religion was no obstacle at all. Maybe they've abandoned that now. They understood right away the significance that RU-486 could have—and they wanted to be a part. A big part.[97]

And so they did. Without the incisive influx of millions from the Rockefeller Foundation—the one-time missions subsidy turned "altruistic" internationalist front—RU-486 would have probably floundered in obscurity until it died a natural death. But with it, the drug seems virtually unstoppable.

THE ISSUE

Hilaire Belloc once said:

> Time after time mankind is driven against the horrid reality of a fallen creation. And time after time mankind must learn the hard lessons of history—the lessons that for some dangerous and awful reason we can't seem to keep in our collective memory.[98]

The proponents of RU-486 abortion say they believe it is merely an issue of reproductive freedom. They say they believe it is an issue of personal choice. They say they believe it is an issue of maternal rights. They say they believe it is an issue of individual privacy. They say they believe it is an issue of comprehensive medical care. They say they believe it is an issue of economic expediency. They say they believe it is a matter of simple altruism.

But that is not true. They know full well that abortion is not an issue at all. An *issue* is something we can reasonably and rationally discuss around a negotiating table. An *issue* is something we can compromise on. It is something that involves give and take. It is something we can ponder, argue, and debate. Indeed, it is something good men and women can legitimately disagree on. We can juggle its niggling little points back and forth. Or we can do nothing at all. We can take it or leave it.

Abortion is none of those things. Instead, it is a matter of life and death. It is a test of faith. It is perhaps the ultimate test of faith in these difficult and complex times—and has been throughout all time. It is the dividing line between two inimical worldviews—between the whole of the Christian faith on the one hand and the Malthusian throwbacks to ancient paganism on the other.

And thus it demands uncompromising, unwavering, and unhesitating faithful action.

> All those who find the Lord, find life. But all those who hate God, love death—injuring themselves in the folly that is sin. (Proverbs 8:35, 36)

4

Witch Doctors

Agrescit Medendo[1]

*The most dangerous form of sentimental debauch is to
give expression to good wishes on behalf of virtue
while you do nothing about it. Justice is not merely
words. It is to be translated into living acts.*[2]

THEODORE ROOSEVELT

*Some praise the balm of Gilead, or man's morality;
many try the Roman salve, or the oil of Babylon; and
others use a cunning ointment mixed by learned
philosophers; but for his own soul's wounds, and for
the hurts of others, the wise man knows but one cure,
and that is given gratis by the Good Physician to all
who ask for it.*[3]

CHARLES H. SPURGEON

JUST outside the Paris laboratory of the Inserm Institute—
where Etienne-Emile Baulieu continues to tinker with more
and more efficient applications of his RU-486 abortifacient—
there is a mammoth granite arch. Dedicated to some long-forgot-
ten Napoleonic triumph, it is an architectural anomaly in an

otherwise sleek and urbane landscape; its ornately fluted rococo design seems entirely out of scale, and its rich alpine solidity seems entirely out of place. It juts up from sheer nothingness, for no apparent reason, at no one's bidding—a gate to nowhere.

In reality, though, it could not be more appropriately or significantly situated. Its static beauty testifies to some terrible continuity between itself and the empty contemporary vulgarity of its surroundings. It is a perfect symbol of the mind-set of Baulieu and his modern medical peers: a door with no house attached.

Marie-Louise Colbert has chosen that empty arch to be the backdrop for her singular crusade. Every day, during her lunch hour, she hands out informational brochures to passersby—brochures that detail the personal hell she and thousands of other women have been subjected to because of what the medical establishment has foisted upon them in the name of progress.

"My experience is not all that unique," she told me. "In fact, it is all too common. More than a thousand women are now taking RU-486 every single week. And the documented risks are multiplying at an astonishing rate. I am utterly horrified. It is so grievous to think that many of them will have to go through what I have been through."

Two years ago Marie-Louise became pregnant. She had just gotten a promotion at the advertising agency where she worked, and though she really wanted to have children someday she and her husband felt they simply could not afford it at the time. So they opted for a chemical abortion. Young, fit, active, and with no health problems whatsoever, she did not foresee how there could possibly be any difficulties. Neither did the doctors at the Paris Bicetre Hospital.

They were wrong.

Marie-Louise was one of the unlucky 5 percent who fail to deliver a dead child after the tedious and painful application of RU-

486 and a prostaglandin. After almost two weeks of agony, bizarre side effects, and debilitating complications, she had to undergo a surgical abortion.

During that procedure her cervix was severely lacerated, and both her uterus and her bowels were punctured. Within just a few hours infection raged through her abdominal cavity. She was immediately put into the critical care unit—where doctors regularly have to tend to the victims of "safe and legal" abortions.[4]

Before her long ordeal was over, she had spent seven weeks in the hospital and had undergone three major surgeries—including a last-ditch-effort hysterectomy.

"No one ever told me about the risks," she said. "No one ever told me about the complications. No one ever told me about the side effects. No one ever told me about fetal development. No one ever told me about anything. During my recovery, when I began to ask nurses and therapists *why* all this had happened to me—*how* it could have happened to me—I was simply told to relax and that the doctors knew what was best for me."

She was outraged. "It was like I was supposed to just accept these consequences as everyday occurrences. Well, maybe they are everyday occurrences for them, but they're not for me."

With tears streaming down her cheeks, she turned a piercing gaze upon me. "And I'm not alone," she said. "That is the worst part of all. I am not alone. There are thousands of other women just like me. That is why I stand here in this archway every day during my lunch hour—to tell them that, in fact, none of us are alone."

She looked away—at nothing in particular—and after a long painful pause said, "I'm twenty-three years old. The only child I will ever bear was killed, and then I was medically mutilated—all in the name of technological progress. I can't let them do this to someone else—not if I can help it."

THE HEALING CENTURY

The advancement of medical technology over the past one hundred years represents one of the greatest episodes of human endeavor. The list of achievements appears to be startlingly impressive.

Thanks to antibiotics such as penicillin, many infectious diseases—including scarlet fever, rheumatic fever, gonorrhea, and meningitis—can now be almost entirely controlled.

Vaccines have saved the lives of millions of children and made such scourges as polio, diphtheria, and smallpox nearly extinct.

Diabetes, gout, arthritis, high blood pressure, emphysema, and other chronic illnesses have become more and more manageable with the help of innumerable innovative treatments.

Countless lifesaving surgical procedures have followed on the heels of the development of sophisticated antiseptics and anesthesias.

In the battle against cancer and heart disease, a phenomenal arsenal of high-tech weaponry has been marshaled—radiation therapy, laser surgery, elemental bombardment, organ transplants, orthoscopic incising, partical transfusions, mechanical prostheses, gene replication, and receptor articulation.

Virtually every malady and condition known to man has faced an unrelenting barrage of new drugs or techniques or operations or therapies or treatments or formulas or procedures. Manned space flights to the moon almost pale in comparison to the flights of fancy that have actually been realized by doctors in search of the sure cure.

Not surprisingly, along with the development of this remarkable technological boom has come a financial boom as well. Medicine is a major growth industry all around the globe.[5] More than a trillion and a half dollars are dedicated to it every year— providing hospitals, pharmaceutical companies, research institutes, and alternative clinics with a lion's share of the world's economic resources.[6]

With that financial clout has come political and cultural clout as well—with almost no outside scrutiny or accountability. To even raise the question of the relative cost, effectiveness, or even desirability of the disease management industry has become practically taboo. According to Sami Ladourvec, a renowned medical researcher at the University of Belgrade:

> The medical establishment has become a kind of modern high priesthood—very nearly unquestioned and unquestionable. Because of its hold over the very lives of people, it is able to boldly exact financial, political, and even social concessions that no other profession would even dream of asking for.[7]

Similarly, Lewis Thomas, the prolific president of the Memorial Sloan-Kettering Cancer Center, has said:

> It seems taken for granted that the technology of medicine simply exists, take it or leave it, and the only major technological problem which policy-makers are interested in is how to deliver today's kind of health care, with equity, to all the people.[8]

As a result, governments without hesitation devote vast sums of their annual budgets to support the medical industry apparatus.[9] Special liability exemptions are granted for its research efforts.[10] Massive proportions of higher education resources are channeled into its development projects.[11] And ancillary support from innumerable service professions and institutions has been spawned— making medicine an unrivaled and sacrosanct sort of techno-industrial complex.[12]

Thus technological health care has been turned into a standardized commodity, a staple, an essential element of modern life.

And as a result it has become one of the wealthiest and most influential forces in our culture—overpowering nearly every other concern.[13]

The question is, has it been worth it?

CURES WORSE THAN DISEASES

While it is generally recognized that medical care probably costs too much—inflation-adjusted expenses have risen more than 500 percent during the last ten years—the common consensus is that despite that solitary drawback, doctors do a pretty good job at what they do.[14]

With nary an exception, people accept as a matter of demonstrable fact that great advances in the medical technology and health care industries have greatly improved our health and well-being. They simply take it for granted that doctors have extended the average life expectancy. They believe with a special ardency that discovering the cures for most diseases is just a matter of time. It is a foregone conclusion for them that prescribed drugs can alleviate the ills of almost any abnormal condition—and that whatever our doctors or pharmacists sell us can and should be taken in good faith.

But none of this is true.

The greatest advances in health care over the past hundred years have been the result of sanitation, hygiene, and nutrition—not medicine or pharmacology. Simple things like a pure water supply, a decent sewage system, and a healthy diet have saved far more lives than open heart surgery or chemotherapy.[15] Brushing teeth, washing hands, and shampooing scalps have affected the well-being of millions more than immunology or neurosurgery.[16]

The plain fact is, there is no empirical evidence that the health status of modern man has significantly improved as a result of the

progress of technological medicine.[17] The average life expectancy
has actually begun to decline.[18] Epidemics still rage uncontrolled.[19]
And human misery remains a mysterious unchecked scourge.[20]
While medicine has undoubtedly tasted some real success in a number of areas, it has hardly lived up to either the claims or the expectations that have been universally attached to it. On the contrary,
as the respected medical ethicist Ivan Illich has revealed, much
modern technological medicine may actually do more harm than
good. "The medical establishment has become a major threat to
health," he says. In fact:

> A vast amount of contemporary clinical care is incidental to the
> curing of disease, but the damage done by medicine to the
> health of individuals and populations is very significant. These
> facts are obvious, well documented, and well repressed.[21]

Illich goes on to assert that:

> The study of the evolution of disease patterns provides evidence
> that during the last century doctors have affected epidemics no
> more profoundly than did mystics during earlier times.
> Epidemics came and went, imprecated by both but touched by
> neither. They are not modified any more decisively by the ritu-
> als performed in medical clinics than by those customary at
> religious shrines.[22]

Amazingly, the most common and dread malady in Western
societies today is iatrogenic—in other words, medically-caused
sicknesses or complications.[23] Not cancer. Not AIDS. Not heart disease. But iatrogenesis. The plethora of therapeutic side effects and
pathogens caused by modern medical technology have reached
pandemic proportions.[24]

Horror stories abound of unnecessary surgeries, operating

room mixups, and procedural errors. Professional callousness, impersonal negligence, and sheer incompetence seem to dominate the clinical environment—perhaps they always have.[25] Worse, bizarre practices reminiscent of Nazi-era medicine—like fetal harvesting, genetic engineering, virtual reality,[26] cryogenics,[27] daeliaforcation,[28] cybernetics,[29] euthanasia, cell reailination,[30] and infanticide—have come back into vogue and have almost become commonplace.[31] But the most troubling aspect of modern medicine is its promiscuous reliance on chemical treatments.

Pharmaceuticals have always been potentially poisonous, but their risks have increased with their potency and widespread use.[32] Every day between 50 and 80 percent of adults in the industrialized West swallow a medically prescribed drug. Some take the wrong drug—either because the doctor wrongly diagnosed the problem, or the pharmacist made a mistake, or the patient picked up the wrong bottle out of the medicine cabinet. Some get an old or contaminated batch of the drug. Some take an inferior counterfeit or generic version. And some take several drugs in dangerous combinations.

There are a number of drugs on the market that are addictive, others mutilating, and others mutagenic—particularly in combination with food coloring or insecticides. Many of them have very little therapeutic value or are entirely unproven but are prescribed nonetheless because of convenience or especially effective marketing by pharmaceutical companies in the medical community.[33]

But even proven drugs can cause grave harm. In some patients, for instance, antibiotics can alter the normal bacterial flora and induce a superinfection, permitting more resistant organisms to proliferate and invade the host. Other drugs contribute to the breeding of drug-resistant strains of bacteria. Subtle new forms of poisoning have thus spread even faster than the bewildering variety and ubiquity of nostrums. Every year more than 7 percent of all non-ambulatory hospital admissions are due to adverse reactions to prescribed drugs.[34]

Pharmaceutical malpractice is especially acute in gynecological medicine—reflecting an overall trend toward the political and economic exploitation of women by the medical industry.[35] In the fevered rush to get various contraceptive and abortifacient drugs to market, women have suffered under the strain of almost unending complications and side effects.[36] In essence, women using birth control have served the industry as guinea pigs—unwitting subjects in prolonged and deathly-dangerous experiments.[37] Today seven of the ten most frequently prescribed drugs in the West are gynecologically related—which is especially frightening in light of the fact that three of the four most frequently performed surgical procedures are also exclusively gynecological—thus making the womb a literal war zone for the practitioners of modern medicine.[38]

Frederick Robbins, a noted figure in pharmacological research, justified the use of unsafe gynecological drugs saying:

> The dangers of overpopulation are so great that we may have to use certain techniques of contraception that may entail considerable risk to the individual woman.[39]

Thus when all is said and done, a woman's health considerations and personal choices take a backseat to the economic, political, and social agenda of the techno-medical industrial complex.

Not surprisingly, the number of medical malpractice suits has soared over the last two decades. It is now estimated that the average doctor will face at least three major lawsuits sometime during his career.[40] But the average gynecologist can expect at least twelve.[41]

Francisco Goya, in *Los Caprichos*—a series of etchings the artist executed in 1786—shows a man asleep at his laboratory desk with his head on his crossed arms while monsters surround him.

The inscription on the desk reads: "*el sueno de la razon produce monstruos*"—literally, "the dreams of reason produce monsters."

Goya knew that medicine, like art, when not in the service of Heaven, is most likely in the service of Hell.

It appears that much of the emphasis of the modern health care industry is on engineering the dreams of reason. And the result is monstrously hellish.

ANOTHER WORLD

It may well be that the damnable failure of modern medicine is much more a maltheory than a malpractice. In other words, the problem with health care is not so much bad technologies as bad philosophies.

Interestingly, those philosophies may arise not so much out of malice and malignancy as out of directionlessness. According to C. Everett Koop, the former Surgeon General of the United States:

> I don't think a medical student is ever told what his mission in life is. Certainly no one ever told me what was expected of me as a lifetime goal in assuming the role of a physician.[42]

Similarly, Sami Ladourvec has said:

> With the subtle secularization and industrialization of medicine, has come a rootlessness, a lack of cohesiveness, and a latitudinarianism. There is no longer a philosophical definition to our profession. The tragic result is that young doctors have no real sense of calling, and they either have to find meaning and purpose in raw financial gain or in some ideological pursuit. What we are seeing then is the inevitable fragmentation of medicine into a thousand cults and sects.[43]

"When you don't have any clear purpose or direction," says entrepreneurial business consultant Charles Handy, "whether it is in a company, a government, a family, or a profession, anything can and will happen—usually it is bad."[44] Indeed, the proliferation of everything from homeopathy and iridology to applied kinesiology and acupuncture under the rubric of modern health care demonstrates that the splintering of medical philosophies has indeed resulted in a splintering of medical practices.[45]

According to Ladourvec, that kind of professional anarchy has very serious consequences for us all:

> In an atmosphere like that, the tools of technology can be very destructive—it is perhaps no less dangerous than if we were to allow every petty Third World tyrant to have access to nuclear weapons.[46]

Of course, the present intellectual schizophrenia is a fairly recent development. Up until this century medicine had a consistent and cohesive philosophical foundation.

The earliest medical guild appeared on the Aegean island of Cos, just off the coast of Asia Minor. Around the time Nehemiah was organizing the post-exilic Jews in Jerusalem to rebuild that city's walls, Aesculapius was organizing the post-exilic Jews on Cos into adept medical specialists—for the first time in history, moving medical healing beyond folk remedies and pagan rituals. It was not long before this elite guild had earned renown throughout the Mediterranean world under the leadership of Hippocrates, son of Panacea, son of Hygeia, son of Aesculapius, son of Hashabia the Hebrew, an exile of fallen Jerusalem.[47]

Thus the great Greek school of healing that laid the foundations of modern medicine—that gave us the Hippocratic Oath and the scientific standards for hygiene, diagnosis, and systematic treatment which form the basis for comprehensive health maintenance—wasn't actually Greek at all. It was Hebrew—the fruit of Biblical faith.[48]

In the centuries that followed, wherever and whenever Biblical faith flourished, so did medicine. The fact is, medicine has always been a special legacy of believers—provoked by Biblical compassion, fueled by Biblical conviction, and guided by Biblical ethics.

When plague and pestilence convulsed the peoples of the past, it was merciful Christians who stood steadfast amidst the terrors establishing hostels, clinics, and ultimately hospitals. Even a cursory survey demonstrates that throughout history Christian nations have always been havens of medical proficiency—guarding the sanctity of life. Whereas in pagan nations, medical technology invariably degenerated into crude superstition. It became just one more bludgeon to exploit the weak, the poor, and the helpless.

It takes more imagination to dismiss the civilization that gave us Stephansdomplatz, Chartres, and Westminster than to accept them. But of course many modern medical practitioners are terribly imaginative.

And so today on the one hand there are doctors who no longer make house calls or sit on the edges of beds because their science has become so institutional, while on the other hand there are doctors who perform occult and cabalistic rites because their science has become so mystical. Either way, their respective practices have ceased to be entirely human—one is black impudence, the other is black nonsense. Both are black magic—an utterly alien rite to the worldview application that gave the profession its earlier greatness.

According to Illich:

Medical procedures turn into black magic when, instead of mobilizing and enlisting responsible participation in the healing process, they transform the sick man into a limp and mystified voyeur of his own treatment. Medical procedures turn into bad philosophy—even bad religion—when they are performed as rituals that focus the entire expectation of the sick on scientific or mystical mechanisms.[49]

Thankfully, there is an ever-growing number of Christian specialists and family practitioners who have not yielded to this awful alchemy.[50] While not disclaiming the very real advances of modern medicine, they are attempting to restore the personal and covenantal dimensions to a trade lost in a New Age cosmos of confusion. Sadly, their finger-in-the-dike vigil is often terribly lonely.[51]

MAGIC

The primary difference between Christianity and paganism is that true religion is a response to truth, but false religion is an attempt to manipulate man and nature—or perhaps even God Himself. Faith aims at God's satisfaction, while faithlessness aims at self-satisfaction.

Throughout the ages faithless men such as Cain have used religion to get what they want (Genesis 4:3-8; Hebrews 11:4; 1 John 3:12). Men such as Balaam have used religion to control circumstances (Numbers 31:16; 2 Peter 2:15; Revelation 2:14). Men such as Korah have used religion to enhance their position (Numbers 16:1-3, 31-35). Cain, Balaam, and Korah all believed in the universal power of certain natural laws or mechanisms. They believed that not only could they manipulate human society and environmental elements with those laws, but that God would also be forced to conform Himself to the desires and demands of men who act in terms of them—that if they would say certain things, do certain things, believe certain things, or act out certain things, God would have to respond. In essence they believed that man controlled his own destiny, using certain rituals, systems, and formulas—like magic—to shape history, to govern society, to change nature, to control mankind, and to manipulate God.

Sadly, men are forever rejecting the sovereignty of God, "going the way of Cain, rushing headlong into the error of Balaam, and perishing in the rebellion of Korah" (Jude 11).

That is the reason statism is so predominant among rebellious men and nations—because if some legal mechanisms can shape history, govern society, change nature, control mankind, and manipulate God, then obviously men can work to institutionalize those mechanisms as some kind of a saving law-order. If certain rituals, systems, and formulas do indeed work like magic, men can erect an oligarchical standard of rule to govern men legalistically—manufacturing salvation by legislation.

That is also why scientism is so predominant today. If some scientific mechanisms can be discovered that will brush aside all of our woes, worries, and wiles, we just might be able to institutionalize those mechanisms as some kind of saving health-order. If certain potions, elixirs, and treatments do indeed work like magic, men can impose an oligarchical standard of vivacity to heal men medically—fabricating salvation by medication.

Of course, the end result of either the magic of statism or the magic of scientism is some inhuman tyranny—running roughshod over the very people they are supposed to save.

The organization and the individual most responsible for the development of RU-486—the World Health Organization (WHO) and Etienne-Emile Baulieu—illustrate that fact with stunning clarity.

THE ORGANIZATION

At the end of the Second World War, the newly convened United Nations approved a joint proposal from Brazil and China that an international health organization should be established. According to Brock Chisholm—a delegate from Canada who would eventually become the director of the new organization—that decision was truly momentous:

> History is studded with critical dates—wars, invasions, revolutions, discoveries, peace treaties—that are firmly implanted in our minds. But the establishment of the World Health Organization may well go down in history as one of the most far-reaching of all international agreements. It will surely be a positive force with broad objectives, reaching forward to embrace nearly all levels of human activity.[52]

Chisholm's almost messianic expectations were apparently shared by the other delegates and thus were reflected in the new organization's charter—which opened with a commitment to nine principles that all the participating nations agreed were "basic to the happiness, harmonious relations, and security of all peoples."[53] Those principles were stated in broad terms and open language:

- "Health is a state of complete physical, mental, and social well-being and not merely the absence of disease or infirmity."
- "The enjoyment of the highest attainable standard of health is one of the fundamental rights of every human being without distinction of race, religion, political belief, economic or social condition."
- "The health of all peoples is fundamental to the attainment of peace and security and is dependent upon the fullest cooperation of individuals and states."
- "The achievement of any State in the promotion and protection of health is of value to all."
- "Unequal development in different countries in the promotion of health and control of disease, especially communicable disease, is a common danger."

- "Healthy development of the child is of basic importance; the ability to live harmoniously in a changing total environment is essential to such development."
- "The extension to all peoples of the benefits of medical, psychological, and related knowledge is essential to the fullest attainment of health."
- "Informed opinion and active cooperation on the part of the public are of the utmost importance in the improvement of the health of the people."
- "Governments have a responsibility for the health of their peoples which can be fulfilled only by the provision of adequate health and social measures."[54]

Early critics claimed that such a charter was:

A magna carta for unrestricted and global meddling; a limitless grant of power to investigate and legislate on almost anything and everything imaginable.[55]

Even its supporters admitted that the new organization had been given extraordinary ambiguous powers. Indeed, Charles A. Winslow of Yale University said, "It would be difficult to imagine a broader charter."[56]

By defining health as "a state of complete physical, mental, and social well-being, and not merely the absence of disease or infirmity," the framers had not only placed conventional medical concerns under the organization's purview, but also such things as housing standards, nutritional balance, economic status, labor relations, environmental concerns, mental and emotional fulfillment, and any and all social, religious, administrative or political conditions that might be construed to affect public health in some way, shape, or form. In fact, it would be difficult to imagine any area of human thought or activity—private or public, individual or collective, local or international—not covered by the juridical authority of the World Health Organization.

Amazingly, the participating nations also pledged to yield the power of enforcement to the new organization. The charter brashly asserts absolute sovereignty in this regard:

> The Health Assembly shall have authority to adopt conventions or agreements with respect to any matter within the competence of the organization.[57]

And since there is virtually no matter which is not within its competence, the organization has a virtual blank check for dictatorial discretion:

> Each member State undertakes that it will, within eighteen months after the adoption by the Health Assembly of a convention or agreement, take action relative to the acceptance of such convention or agreement. Each member shall notify the director-general of the action taken.[58]

Establishing its international headquarters in Geneva, with six regional offices spread out around the globe—in Washington, Manila, New Delhi, Copenhagen, Alexandria, and Brazzaville—the organization quickly fulfilled its founders' expectations and grew to become one of the largest and richest cultural forces the world has ever known.[59] And, today, with a budget of more than one and a half billion dollars a year[60] and activities in some one hundred and sixty-six nations,[61] the organization enjoys more prestige and power than ever before.[62]

Though its activities through the years have included a variety of legitimate health-care concerns ranging from pure water supplies and adequate modern sanitation to malarial infection and AIDS transmission, senior WHO staffers have always placed a heavy emphasis on socio-behavioral issues. Accordingly, a special objective of the agency has always been to provoke changes in moral and sexual ethics. Thus, according to Chisholm:

> The basic psychological distortion in every civilization of which we know anything capable of producing ill health is morality— the concept of good and evil with which to keep children under control, with which to prevent free thinking, and with which to impose loyalties.[63]

Later he would comment:

> I think that there is no doubt that the idea of sin creates much havoc in our relationships with other cultures. We must remember that it is only in some cultures that sin exists. For instance, the Eskimos didn't have this concept until quite recently. Now they have; they caught it from us. They were formerly in a state of innocence, but they had to be made to feel sinful so they could be controlled.[64]

The mission of the World Health Organization would be to remove "such debilitating obstacles" to "mental health" from the face of the earth. And such unambiguous animosity toward traditional values has indeed been systemized through the years in innumerable programs and projects. For example:

- In Communist China, the organization was instrumental in launching a brutal, no-holds-barred, one-child-per-couple government policy.[65]
- Nearly one hundred million forced abortions, mandatory sterilizations, and coercive infanticides later,[66] WHO continues to maintain that the totalitarian government's genocidal approach to population control is a "model of efficiency."[67]

- It has fought to maintain independent international funding of the Chinese operation[68] and has continued to increase its own funding and program support involvement[69] despite widespread reports of human rights atrocities.[70]
- Similar draconian measures have been implemented at the organization's behest in Bangladesh, Zaire, Sierra Leone, Ethiopia, India, Pakistan, and Indonesia.[71] Providing each of these countries with detailed restraints and quotas, suggested compulsory incentives and disincentives, and assistance in circumventing public opinion and moral opposition, the WHO has taken the lead in the international campaign to crush the rights of women to choose if and when they will have children.[72]

The pinnacle of this anti-Christian assault against the family has been the organization's rabid commitment to RU-486 and other abortifacient drugs. From the beginning it was the WHO that provided the funding,[73] the research facilities,[74] the political pull,[75] and the public relations expertise[76] necessary to insure the drug's success. According to the organization's Division of Public Information, "The acceptance of RU-486 is a major objective of the WHO. We are prepared to spare no expense to insure its deployment."[77]

The leaders of the organization understand only too clearly that the drug is the very magic they have been yearning for—a tool to effect and control social, political, and cultural transformation. It is thus a natural obsession for the progenitor of iatrogenic medicine.

THE INDIVIDUAL

Etienne-Emile Blum was born in 1926 into a close-knit Jewish family in France. His childhood was serene and uneventful—until the advent of the Second World War and the collapse of the French government. Fleeing to Grenoble for safety, the family changed its name to Baulieu, and the young boy joined the Francs-Tireurs et Partisans Francais—which were the irregular resistance forces controlled by the Communists. He spent most of the war breaking windows in the Gestapo militia barracks and soaking up the rudiments of Marxist ideology. After the liberation of Annecy, he joined a regular battalion on the alpine front for a short time, but before he saw any real action, the war was over.

With the encouragement of his Communist comrades, he went to medical school and took an almost immediate interest in birth control. It was an issue regularly discussed among the *Auberges de Jeunesse*—the Communist youth cells which were the precursors to the revolution of May 1968. Several of the ardent young strategists believed the only way to break the current cultural consensus of Christian morality—which they correctly believed was the chief obstacle to totalitarian control—was through a direct interference with the family structure. Birth control could very well be the wedge they needed. So Baulieu made it his speciality.

After graduating from medical school, he tried to get a visa to come to the United States to study at Columbia University with Seymour Lieberman and Gregory Pincus—two of the early sex hormone researchers sponsored by Planned Parenthood, the Rockefeller Foundation, and the World Health Organization—but he was initially denied entry because of his Communist affiliations. He was not easily put off, and he hounded immigration for months.

His persistence ultimately paid off, and he was able to join the pioneer work on the contraceptive pill—which was then being tested in Puerto Rico among underprivileged women and girls. From Pincus he not only learned the science of child limitation, he learned the language of revolution. That experience set him on his life course.

Shortly thereafter, Baulieu returned to France, where he began his long association with Jean-Claude Roussel and Edouard Sakiz—

principals in the Roussel-Uclaf pharmaceutical conglomerate. The company had nurtured an abiding interest in human anti-hormones for some time. Interestingly, so had its sister company and eventual corporate parent, Hoechst, which after a hasty post-war reorganization had succeeded I. G. Farben—the maker of the Zyklon B gas used at Auschwitz and other Nazi extermination centers.

Irony and paradox are the inevitable consequences of life in the fallen world. But here they are especially manifest. Baulieu, as a Jew, was overturning the foundations of medical ethics established by Jews in antiquity (Hippocrates *et al.*). And Baulieu was employed by the company that supplied gas to exterminate his people in World War II.

When RU-486 came under development, Baulieu recalled all the political and public relations skills he had learned from Pincus and launched into a novel crusade. It was to be both a positive and negative campaign—to promote his drug but also to stymie what he called the "horrific influence" of "fanatic moralists" and the "obscene sway" of "fundamentalists" and "right-wing Protestants and Catholics."[78] "I really don't see a division between politics, industry, and medicine," he said. "Each mechanism helps to contribute to the overall goal. I just do whatever it takes to win."

That's magic. And that's scary.

THE ENTERPRISE

It is difficult to live in the same town with a man who lives in a different universe. Opposing worldviews are not just contrary opinions, they are contrary realities.

Whenever any problem arises, the advocates of one sort of magic or another—whether they are organizations or individuals—rush to the bar with a whole series of self-conceived or self-perceived procedures, systems, rules, regulations and laws.

That is the way of the modern world.

That is the way of technological medicine.

That is the way of tyranny.

But the enterprise of the Christian is to face problems through the lens of God's own revelation:

> All Scripture is given by inspiration of God, and is profitable for doctrine, for reproof, for correction, for instruction in righteousness, that the man of God may be complete, thoroughly equipped for every good work. (2 Timothy 3:16, 17)

To attempt to reform injustices, heal infirmities, or solve dilemmas without taking heed to the clear instruction of Scripture is utter foolishness (Romans 1:18-23). It is to invite inadequacy and incompetency (Deuteronomy 28:15). All such attempts are doomed to frustration and failure (Deuteronomy 30:15-20). Magic simply cannot and will not work—whether it is scientific or mystical—because magic is out of touch with reality (Ephesians 5:6). It is fraught with fantasy (Colossians 2:8).

Only the Bible can tell us of things as they really are (Psalm 19:7-11). Only the Bible faces reality squarely, practically, completely, and honestly (Deuteronomy 30:11-14). Thus only a Biblical worldview can provide genuine solutions to the problems that plague mankind.

Until the practitioners of modern medicine comprehend that reality, they will be little better than witch doctors. Perhaps T. S. Eliot had that in mind when he lamented:

> *Where is the life we have lost in living?*
> *Where is the wisdom we have lost in knowing?*
> *The cycles of heaven in twenty centuries,*
> *Bring us farther from God and nearer to dust.*[79]

5

The Glitz Blitz

Ad Capandum Vulgus[1]

It is the profoundest question any philosopher has ever pondered: why are otherwise sane citizens wowed by the unabashed foolishness of the press, the shameful hucksterism of the profiteer, and the blatant concupiscence of the powerful. Woe to the republic that falls prey to their skillful commerce.[2]

THEODORE ROOSEVELT

A lantern is of no use to a bat, and good teaching is lost on the man who will not learn. Reason is folly with the unreasonable.[3]

CHARLES H. SPURGEON

THE great American novelist, essayist, and humorist Mark Twain once said:

It is by the goodness of God that in the West we have those three unspeakably precious things: freedom of speech, freedom of conscience, and the prudence never to practice either of them.[4]

Apparently what he intended in jest, the international news media intends in earnest. Worked into a blathering bother over the RU-486 controversy, those diligent souls who style themselves as the keepers of the keys to truth and justice opine almost daily the imprudence of concerned citizens who might have the temerity and audacity to exercise their freedoms of speech and conscience to oppose RU-486's testing, approval, and distribution. In obvious displeasure, they have unleashed their ire on any and all who might question their wisdom on the subject.

Just ask Bob Ramada.

Bob is the vice-president of marketing for a major daily newspaper in a large metropolitan region. He is also a committed Christian. Recently the editorial page of his paper ran a commentary that heralded RU-486 as "the answer to the abortion controversy." Resorting to a disingenuous tabloid journalism so patently devoid of fact that even the *National Enquirer* would have blushed with shame, the editorial bungled data, engaged in hyperbole, and repeated obvious distortions. Typically it also railed against "the schizophrenia of the so-called pro-life movement."

Bob was outraged. "I certainly don't begrudge the paper taking a strong advocacy position on the subject—no matter how much I may disagree with it," he told me at the time. "But what really bothers me about this was the complete lack of professional integrity that the editorial displayed. The least they could do is get their facts straight."

Bob decided that he needed to make a public response. "After all, my name is on the masthead. I felt like it was my responsibility to offer a more balanced perspective."

Taking great pains not to repeat the oft repeated errors of fact and judgment about the drug, Bob pulled together much of the available published material on RU-486. "I knew it was bad before, but I really had no idea how bad. Quite frankly, I was shocked that anyone in his right mind could possibly support this thing."

Armed now with the facts, Bob wrote a reasoned response. The editorial page editor was impressed. He printed it as a very prominent op-ed article. A few letters—pro and con—came into the offices over the next few days. And then, almost as quickly as it had begun, the controversy disappeared.

At least that is what Bob thought.

Actually several people were working behind the scenes to punish him for his stance.

A week after the first editorial appeared, two of Bob's employees filed a formal complaint against him with the senior management of the paper. They accused him of "proselytizing" on the job, of "unruly and prejudicial behavior," and of "incompatibility with female employees." Although he had doubled the number of ad pages in just three years and had built an unwaveringly loyal sales team, he was also accused of "failing to properly execute" his "job responsibilities."

More than two months of tribulation then followed. Bob had to undergo several intensive reviews with both his immediate supervisors and the corporate officers. He was temporarily relieved of his duties in the marketing department. And he was told that he would probably have to transfer to another city, in order to "get a fresh start."

"I really couldn't believe this was happening to me," he said. "It was like living a nightmare. The tension around the office was so thick, you could cut it with a knife—but no one was willing to admit the whole thing had been caused by my editorial."

Eventually his publisher admitted to Bob that indeed the editorial had provoked the crisis. "But he told me the paper wasn't actually trying to censor my views—it was just trying keep a good harmonious working atmosphere in the building. The bottom line, he said, was that even if I was totally in the right, I had made things really unpleasant around the office. And that was unacceptable."

Bob was stunned. He suddenly realized he was suffering through an ordeal of professional persecution, not so much because he had violated an unwritten code of pro-abortion orthodoxy, but because he had dared to violate the delicate balance of social etiquette. "As far as my boss was concerned," he said, "truth was not nearly as important as gentility."

There is perhaps nothing more menacing or dangerous today than the exaltation of secondary matters of conduct at the expense of primary matters of dogma. In fact, there is only one thing worse than the contemporary weakening of major morals, and that is the contemporary strengthening of minor morals. Thus Bob discovered that it is a more heinous offense to be accused of having bad taste or bad timing than to be accused of having bad ethics or bad behavior.

THE BIAS CLICHÉ

To accuse the media of bias has become an almost indisputable truism. Christian media pioneer Marlin Maddoux stated the obvious when he said that after a comprehensive analysis of American network news coverage, he was forced to conclude:

> There wasn't a nickle's worth of difference among the *Big Three*—ABC, CBS, and NBC. The stories were basically the same; the bias in their coverage was the same. It became frighteningly clear that the television screen was dominated by the radical left. And opposing views were virtually closed out.[5]

Even members of the media elite readily admit that the charge of bias is not at all unfounded. NBC's Robert Bazell asserts that "objectivity is a fallacy. Journalism is almost always about a point of view."[6] Independent producer Linda Ellerbee agrees: "We report news, not truth. There is no such thing as objectivity. Any reporter who tells you he's objective is lying to you."[7] And Geraldo Rivera has argued that objectivity "was invented by journalism schools. It has very little to do with real life."[8]

The reason for this is actually quite simple: the media—like any other discipline or profession—operates according to its own perspectives and presuppositions. It has its own unique agenda. Herbert Gans, a renowned media analyst, has said:

> Journalism is, like sociology, an empirical discipline. As a result, the news consists not only of the findings of empirical inquiry, but also of the concepts and methods which go into that inquiry, the assumptions that underlie those concepts and methods, and even a further set of assumptions, which could then be tested empirically if journalists had the time.[9]

When it comes to the abortion issue, that ready bias is especially evident. Even if the famous Rothman-Lichter survey had not told us that more than 90 percent of newsmen today are personally pro-abortion,[10] we might have guessed it. After all, if it looks like a duck, walks like a duck, and quacks like a duck, it is probably a duck.

Thus, as the *Los Angeles Times* reported:

> It's not surprising that some abortion-rights activists would see journalists as their natural allies. Most major newspapers support abortion rights on their editorial pages, and two major media studies have shown that eighty to ninety percent of U.S. journalists personally favor abortion rights. Moreover some reporters participated in a big abortion rights march in Washington last year, and the American Newspaper Guild, the union that represents news and editorial employees at many

major papers, has officially endorsed freedom of choice in abortion decisions.[11]

The article went on to assert:

> Responsible journalists do try to be fair, and many charges of bias in abortion coverage are not valid. But careful examination of stories published and broadcast reveals scores of examples, large and small, that can only be characterized as unfair to the opponents of abortion, either in content, tone, choice of language, or prominence of play.[12]

The coverage of the RU-486 controversy demonstrates that bias only too clearly. A survey of more than two hundred published articles in magazines, newspapers, and periodicals in Great Britain and America over the past year revealed that only twenty-two mentioned the serious complications and side effects caused by the drug, only nineteen quoted pro-life sources or experts, and a mere nine conveyed any negative connotations whatsoever.[13]

The fact is, the media's Milli Vanilli-like lip-synching of the pro-abortion party line provides stark evidence that it has tossed any semblance of impartiality or objectivity to the four winds.

But that is not the most disturbing aspect of the media's coverage of the issue. Bias is a fairly straightforward vice. What is even more insidious than an absence of factual objectivity is an absence of professional integrity—journalists have indulged in ventriloquism instead of oratory.

The essence of science is precision. The essence of sentiment is presumption. Because the media has difficulty distinguishing one from the other, it is both precise and presumptuous—but about exactly the wrong things. When it comes to their abortifacient coverage, the media has been very scientific and sociological about sentimental things, but very sentimental about scientific and socio-logical things.

They have, in short, not checked the facts, not verified the data, and not understood the issues. They have invariably taken the easy way out—by using news releases from pro-abortion lobbyists and publicists and simply adding their byline.

Instead of working harder, they shouted louder. Instead of striving for professional excellence, they have settled for profes-sional expediency. Instead of attempting to grasp their subject mat-ter, they have grasped at straws—and straw men.

That kind of dull dishonesty is either a sign of faulty discipline or faulty ethics—or maybe both.

MOUNTING THE CAMPAIGN

Speaking at an important contraceptive technologies conference recently, RU-486 strategist Marie Bass crowed that "press cover-age really is good, if you think about it—sometimes I worry that it's almost too good." The major media outlets, she confided, had for the most part entirely misunderstood the safety, complexity, and mechanism of the drug. And ironically, that was good news. Bass said she almost felt like celebrating.[14]

She had every right to. That happy misunderstanding, after all, was due in great part to her own expert effort to shape and coor-dinate press coverage of the drug.

In late 1988 Bass & Howes, a high-powered Washington, D.C., lobbying firm, formed the Reproductive Health Technologies Project. A loose coalition of international pro-abortion organiza-tions, it acts as a clearinghouse for information on RU-486 and as the command center for the dissemination of that information to the media.

Marie Bass was at one time the political director of the

National Abortion Rights Action League. Her partner, Joanne Howes, was at one time Planned Parenthood's chief lobbyist in Washington. Together they bring excellent credentials to their job of sanitizing the public perception of pharmaceutical child-killing.

Early on they developed a five-fold strategy to hasten media acceptance of RU-486:

- "Emphasize the possibility that the drug could very well end the whole public abortion struggle by making clinic protests obsolete."
- "Emphasize the dearth of other contraceptive options available—particularly in comparison with what is available in other parts of the world."
- "Emphasize the issues of privacy, ease, safety, choice, and freedom, rather than of abortion and politics."
- "Emphasize the possibility of other medical benefits of the drug, such as treatment of breast cancer and Cushings Syndrome."
- "Emphasize the threat to the freedom of ongoing medical research that a rejection of the drug might bring."[15]

Apparently sometime thereafter Bass and Howes began to supply key media contacts with a series of carefully developed press kits highlighting each emphasis. The kits included sample stories, charts, graphs, photos, and interviews.

Charles Durran, a reporter for a major daily newspaper in the Midwest, told me: "Those press kits were impressive. In fact, they were a lazy reporter's gold mine. Everything you needed for a really fantastic story—or series of stories—was right there at your fingertips. I don't think I've ever seen anything like it."

Before long stories began appearing in newspapers and magazines all over the U.S. and Britain. Many of them were rumored to bear a striking resemblance to the materials in the press kits, and some were actually copied verbatim.[16]

Time, Newsweek, The Economist, and virtually every major

daily newspaper began to trumpet the five emphases that Bass and Howes had outlined. As if on cue, they quoted the various tenets of the credo without a hint of incredulity.

They claimed the drug was safe.[17] They claimed it was easy to use.[18] They claimed it could short-circuit all the political animosity.[19] They claimed it could cure all manner of other ills.[20] They claimed it was a litmus test for scientific freedom.[21] And they claimed it was merely an advanced contraceptive—and everybody knows that only religious cranks and impotent curmudgeons could possibly be against that.[22]

Of course, such fictions rank right up there with Elvis sightings, Martian landings, Beatles reunions, and miracle-product commercials. But the tragedy is not just that the stories were untrue, but that they were cribbed from someone else's script. The media is so lame and helpless in this matter that it cannot even make up its own lies—it is forced to borrow them from others. The only thing worse than getting a failing grade on an exam is cheating to do it.

Such poor deportment is even beneath hypocrisy. After all, hypocrisy is the homage which error pays to truth. But uninformed sloth pays homage to no one and no thing.

THE MEDIA IS THE STORY

More than sixty years ago Walter Lippman made a painfully clear distinction between news and truth. He said:

> The function of news is to signalize an event; the function of truth is to bring to light the hidden facts, to set them into relation with each other, and make a picture of reality on which men can act.[23]

According to Lippman, the differences between news and truth stem not so much from the inadequacies of journalists, but "from the exigencies of the news business, which limits the time, space, and resources that can be allotted to any single story."[24]

He concluded that if the public required "a more truthful interpretation of the world they lived in, they would have to depend on institutions other than the press."[25]

Journalists then, are essentially in the entertainment business. And often they make up their script as they go along—creating news according to their own whims and fancies. As Francis Schaeffer pointed out in his watershed work *How Should We Then Live?*:

> There are certain news organizations, newspapers, news magazines, wire services, and news broadcasts which have the ability to generate news. They are the newsmakers, and when an item appears in them it becomes the news.[26]

The opportunity for, and in fact the inevitability of, manipulation in such a situation is frightening. Schaeffer argued that the media, especially modern network television, manipulate viewers by their normal mode of operation:

> Many viewers seem to assume that when they have seen something on TV, they have seen it with their own eyes. It makes the viewer think he has actually been on the scene. He knows, because his own eyes have seen. He has the impression of greater direct objective knowledge than ever before. For many, what they see on television becomes more true than what they see with their eyes in the external world. But this is not so, for one must never forget that every television minute has been edited. The viewer does not see the event. He sees an edited form of the event. It is not the event which is seen, but an edited symbol or an edited image of the event. An aura and illusion of objectivity and truth is built up, which could not be totally the case even if the people shooting the film were completely

neutral. The physical limitations of the camera dictate that only one aspect of the total situation is given. If the camera were aimed ten feet to the left or ten feet on the right, an entirely different "objective story" might come across. And, on top of that, the people taking the film and those editing it often do have a subjective viewpoint that enters in. When we see a political figure on TV, we are not seeing the person as he necessarily is; we are seeing, rather, the image someone has decided we should see.[27]

In his scathing critique of ethics in journalism, *The News at Any Cost*, Tom Goldstein suggests that not only are reporters the "kingmakers" and "kingbreakers" of our day, they are the "unacknowledged legislators" of our none too pluralistic society.[28]

He says they shape crucial cultural mores, affect the outcome of political contests, create the parameters of public issues, unveil hidden truths—whether true or not—and dictate the social agenda, all on a two-hour deadline. They function not only as the judge, jury, and executioner in the courtroom drama of life, but also as both public defender and criminal prosecutor.

Such power should not be taken lightly. It colors everything it touches. And when that power is cavalierly couched in sluggardly bamboozlement, it is all the more frightening.

When pride comes, then comes shame; but with the humble is wisdom. The integrity of the upright will guide them, but the perversity of the unfaithful will ultimately destroy them. (Proverbs 11:2, 3)

PART III

AGAINST THE TIDE

All these blatant sham reformers, in the name of a new morality, preach the old, old vice and self-indulgence which rotted out first the moral fiber and then even the external greatness of Greece and Rome.[1]

THEODORE ROOSEVELT

The prejudice of the true reformer shuts up many eyes in total darkness. He knows already: he is positive and can swear to it, and it is no use you arguing. He has made up his mind, and it did not take him long, for there is very little of it, but when he has said a thing he sticks to it like cobbler's wax. He is wiser than seven men who can render a reason. He is as positive as if he had been on the other side of the curtain and looked into the backyard of the universe. He talks as if he carried all knowledge in his waistcoat pocket, like a peppermint lozenge. Those who like may try to teach him, but I don't care to hold up a mirror to a mole.[2]

CHARLES H. SPURGEON

6

Fin de Siecle

In Limine[3]

The foes of our own household are our worst enemies; and we can oppose them, not only by exposing them and denouncing them, but by constructive work in planning and building reforms which shall take into account both the economic and the moral factors in human advance. We in America can attain our great destiny only by service; not by rhetoric, and above all not by insincere rhetoric, and that dreadful mental double-dealing and verbal juggling which makes promises and repudiates them, and says one thing at one time, and the directly opposite thing at another time. Our service must be the service of deeds.[4]

THEODORE ROOSEVELT

Those who are quick to promise are generally slow to perform. They promise mountains and perform molehills. He who gives you fair words and nothing more feeds you with an empty spoon. People don't think much of a man's piety when his promises are like pie-crust: made to be broken.[5]

CHARLES H. SPURGEON

Ever since men first learned to measure the passing of time, the *fin de siecle*—or the end of the century—has been filled with expectation and portent. Every culture across the globe has invariably attached special significance to the fact that another hundred years have passed. Some because they thought the earth was coming to an end. Some because they thought the earth was coming to a beginning. But all because they thought the earth was coming to *something*—perhaps even something significantly new and different.

As we approach the end of the twentieth century—and the second millennium since Christ—all those primordial fears, foibles, fancies, and fascinations seem to have redoubled their hold on the attentions of the wise and the foolish alike.

As at the end of the fourth century, men are frightened by the movements of perceived barbarians pouring over once-safe borders with an alarming prolificacy and profligacy.

As at the end of the thirteenth century, men are unsettled by the specter of unchecked plagues rampaging through the population.

As at the end of the fifteenth century, men are uncertain about those things men are usually most certain of—doctrines and dogmas. Their careless admixture of faith and faithlessness has wrought remonstrance, schism, confusion, and inquisition.

As at the end of the eighteenth century, men are shaken by the terrible swiftness of geo-political change—by the revolutionary emergence of startling new alliances, the stirring of age-old animosities, and the plotting of fierce contemporary conspiracies.

The more things change, the more they stay the same.

Because of the obvious parallels, the *fin de siecle* with which our own epoch is most often compared is the end of the tenth century—the culmination of the first Christian millennium.

Then, like now, the speculations of men ran to the frantic and the frenetic. Ecstatic eschatalogical significance was read into every change of any consequence—be it of the weather or of the government. Apocalyptic reticence was chided as faithlessness, while practical intransigence was enshrined as faithfulness. Fantastic common wisdom replaced ordinary common sense, and plain selfish serenity replaced plain selfless civility.

According to legend, that *fin de siecle* witnessed a frenzied, catastrophic effect on the culture:

> New Year's Eve 999, found Christians everywhere in decrepit churches and chapels, awaiting with utmost anxiety whatever the pregnant darkness would bring forth on the stroke of midnight. The suspense of that hour united Christendom in a single community of faith and fear. From Gibraltar to the Baltic, from the English Channel to the Bosporus, from Rome to Constantinople to Jerusalem, the fearful and the faithful gathered their loved ones about them and looked up expectantly toward the celestial vault of the medieval heavens.[6]

Apparently all of the experts were fully convinced that the end was nigh unto them. They had examined all the data—from the Scriptures to the state of affairs around the known world—and were sufficiently persuaded that judgment was near. They worked the populace into a panic.

Of course, their prognostications were wrong:

> When nothing remarkable happened, when the world entered intact upon the year 1000, Sylvester II at his special midnight Mass in Rome turned to the astonished congregation, who lifted their voices to the Lord in the *Te Deum* and hallelujah choruses while clocktowers chimed in the second Christian millennium and bells rang out from all the steeples.[7]

But the people were not merely relieved. They took their new lease on life as a mandate to make a difference in their old tired medieval world:

> Grand sighs of relief became even grander breaths of fresh air as people turned to the rebuilding of the dilapidated chapels, the foundation of monasteries, the creation of Romanesque cathedrals, until the landscape was cloaked in a white mantle of churches. Hungary, Poland and Russia converted to the True Faith in one miraculous gasp. European society, redeemed and transformed, expanded outward under full sails, soon unfurling crusader flags to reclaim Jerusalem from the heathens. Viking raiders vanished into thin northern air, the international climate softened, and sweet winds blew across the wilderness where serfs energetically cleared away first growth for a surging population bound now for that series of renaissances which would propel them into modernity. If ostensibly anti-climactic, the calendrical millennium turned out to have been extraordinarily convenient, a supernally notable year in which the West, after the doldrums of the Dark Ages, at last shook off the reins of barbarians who had not so much succeeded the classical world as ridden roughshod over it.[8]

So as it turned out, that *fin de siecle* was not an *annus terribilis*—a year of horrors—as everyone who was anyone had expected. Rather it was an *annus mirabilis*—a year of marvels.

What made the difference? Was it merely the turning of the page of the calendar? What translated the gloom and doom of that generation's best and brightest into the dawning of a new hope? Was it the razzle-dazzle hat trick of exchanging zeros for nines on the ledger board?

No.

In the end, that *fin de siecle* came and went like all the others had—a mere backdrop to the real drama of green grocers, village cobblers, next-door neighbors, and grandfathers. Despite all the hype, hoopla, and hysteria, the ordinary people who tend their gardens and raise their children and perfect their trades and mind their businesses simply went on with life. Thus the paradoxical convulsion of that time was not manifest in what happened between two dates, but what happened between two peoples—between the eponymous and the anonymous, between the profound and the simple, between the wise made foolish and the foolish made wise.

In fact, that is the great lesson of each *fin de siecle*—throughout all of history, not just those of the tenth and twentieth centuries. It is simply that ordinary people are ultimately the ones who determine the outcome of human events—not kings and princes, not masters and tyrants, not even clocks and calendars. It is that laborers and workmen, cousins and acquaintances can upend the expectations of the brilliant and the glamorous, the expert and the meticulous. It is that plain folks, simple people, can literally change the course of history—because they are the stuff of which history is made. They are the ones who make the world go round.

EXTRAORDINARY ORDINARINESS

G . K. Chesterton said: "The most extraordinary thing in the world is an ordinary man and an ordinary woman and their ordinary children. For indeed, the first shall be last and the last shall be first."

There is something extraordinary going on as we approach the *fin de siecle* precisely because the most significant players on the next world's stage today are so fiercely ordinary. As Chesterton points out, that irony, that paradox, that remarkable reversal is woven into the very fabric of God's good providence in the world.

Because some people cannot comprehend that, they condemn it. The more things change, the more they stay the same.

Christ was once asked about the composition of His extraordinary coming Kingdom. He answered that it will be terribly ordinary:

And Jesus was passing through one city and village to another, teaching, and proceeding on His way to Jerusalem. And someone said to Him: "Lord, are there just a few who are being saved?" And He answered and said to them: "Strive to enter by the narrow door; for many, I tell you, will seek to enter and will not be able. Once the head of the house gets up and shuts the door, and you begin to stand outside and knock on the door, saying, 'Lord open up to us!' then He will answer and say to you, 'I do not know you or where you are from.' Then you will begin to say, 'We ate and drank in Your presence, and You taught in our streets;' and He will say, 'I tell you, I do not know you; depart from Me, all you evildoers.' There will be weeping and gnashing of teeth there when you see Abraham, Isaac, Jacob, and all the prophets in the Kingdom of God, but you yourselves being cast out. Meanwhile, they will come from east and west, and from north and south, and will recline at My table in the Kingdom. And behold, the first shall be last and the last shall be first." (Luke 13:22-30)

When He spoke these words Jesus was on His way to His crucifixion at Jerusalem, and He was met by someone who wanted to know how numerous the company of the saved will be. In two respects, our Lord's answer took unexpected turns.

In the first place He transformed a theological debating point into a personal challenge, immediately pressing the practical implications of the gospel. The questioner asked about a vague and theoretical "them," but Jesus answered with a direct and probing "you."

Secondly, Jesus answered by addressing not the *number* of the saved, but the *identity* of the saved.

This must have startled His interrogator. You see, the Pharisees and Sadducees of the day were obsessed with their pedigree. They were the "children of promise," after all. They were the "heirs of salvation." They knew beyond any shadow of a doubt that they were in like flint. Their only questions concerning the Kingdom were, would God allow any others to taste eternal reward, and if so, how many?

Here Jesus completely upended their expectations. He told them that their pedigree, their proximity, their privilege, and their prominence would be no assurance of a place at the great banqueting table of the Lord. Instead, only those whom He knows, and who know Him, can rest in confident security—and they may very well come from the four ends of the earth. The proud will be cast down, He says, while the humble will be exalted. Those with positions of influence and power will be disregarded, while the despised and rejected will be honored and lifted up. The first shall be last, and the last shall be first.

Of such is the Kingdom. The Bible is full to overflowing with illustrations of that kind of radical reversal, that kind of Kingdom paradox.

- Cain was the firstborn son of Adam and thus the natural heir to all privilege and promise. But it was his younger brother Abel who found favor in God's eyes, and it was his still younger brother Seth who inherited the family blessing and bore the messianic lineage.

- Japheth was the firstborn son of Noah and thus the natural heir to all privilege and promise. But it was his younger brother Shem who inherited the family blessing and bore the messianic lineage.

- Ishmael was the firstborn son of Abraham and thus the natural heir to all privilege and promise. But it was his younger brother Isaac who inherited the family blessing and bore the messianic lineage.

- Esau was the firstborn son of Isaac and thus the natural heir to all privilege and promise. But it was his younger brother Jacob who inherited the family blessing and bore the messianic lineage.

- Reuben was the firstborn son of Jacob and thus the natural heir to all privilege and promise. But it was his younger brother Judah who inherited the family blessing and bore the messianic lineage.

- Eliab was the firstborn son of Jesse and thus the natural heir to all privilege and promise. But it was his younger brother David who inherited the family blessing and bore the messianic lineage.

- Absalom was the firstborn son of David and thus the natural heir to all privilege and promise. But it was his younger brother Solomon who inherited the family blessing and bore the messianic lineage.

Again and again God demonstrates this basic principle of the Kingdom: the weak in Abram's camp overwhelmed the strong in Chedolaomer's camp (Genesis 14); the few in Gideon's army defeated the many in the Midianite army (Judges 7); David faced down Goliath (1 Samuel 17); Elijah stood against Ahab (1 Kings 16); Daniel shut the mouths of both lions and liars (Daniel 6); shepherds and fig pickers were transformed into prophets before kings (Acts 7).

God shames the wise and upholds the foolish (1 Corinthians 1:26-29). He condemns the Pharisee but forgives the publican (Luke 18:10-14). He brings low the great and promotes the obscure (1 Peter 5:5-7). He makes His power manifest not in our strengths, gifts, and abilities, but in our weaknesses, foibles, and failures (2 Corinthians 12:9, 10). God makes something extraordinary out of the ordinary (Hebrews 11:32-40). The first shall be last, and the last shall be first (Luke 13:30).

Though this is one of the primary themes in Scripture, Christ's contemporaries had a difficult time comprehending it. And quite frankly, so do we. God's ways of doing things continually catch us by surprise. God's ways are mysterious to us simply because His ways are not our ways (Isaiah 55:8, 9).

We are obsessed with prominence. We are impressed by fame

and celebrity. How many times have you heard someone say: "O my, if so and so were only a Christian, just imagine what good he could do; just imagine the impact he could make."

Well, the fact is, God uses the ordinary to do the extraordinary. He uses the weak, the afflicted, the common, the mundane, the foolish, the poor, the lonely, the broken, and the humble.

The great eighteenth-century historian Thomas Carlyle wrote in his remarkable essay *Sartor Restartus*:

> Fame is a bewildering, inextricable jungle of delusions, confusions, falsehoods, and absurdities covering the whole field of life. Such misworships and misbeliefs is the furthest thing from greatness and success and is in fact, inimicable to it.[9]

Similarly Hilaire Belloc, in his entertaining critique of French renaissance poetry, *Avril*, wrote:

> Fame is a toy. Its judgment is this: that most of those, having done great things of a good sort, have not fame. And most of those that have fame have done but little things and most of them evil. Old men know this well: there is a vast difference between such mere celebrity and true greatness. Ordinariness is the greatest greatness of all.[10]

Jesus tells us that the Kingdom is rooted in a radical reversal of the common wisdom. He tells us that we may find the heroic in the mundane, not in the profane. We may find glory in commonness, not in prominence.

THE LIGHT OF LIGHT

In the present struggle for sanity, safety, and subsistence—in this battle for life—the most potent weapons we have in our arsenal are the most mundane. Unadorned ordinariness is the secret power that the minions in the political-medical-pharmaceutical establishment most dread.

That is the brilliance of grass-roots activity—it is brilliant precisely because it is mundane. A community's strength is not in its leaders—it is in its followers. The real decision-makers in any culture are the anonymous plodders who are secretly the heroes of history by virtue of their consistent attention to the details that actually matter—loving their wives, enjoying their children, and helping their neighbors. Thus the masters of the universe are not muscle-bound Greek gods come down from Olympus. They are ordinary folks like you and me who know and trust and follow the true God.

Simple people doing simple things is all it takes.

There are a number of simple things that simple people can do about the threat to our health, our families, and our civilization posed by RU-486 and similar abortifacient drugs.

- *We can do our homework—and then spread the word.* We can get our facts straight and then tell as many of our friends and neighbors as we possibly can. One of the reasons so many people are either supportive or ambivalent toward RU-486 is simply that they have never heard the truth about the drug. Even the smothering media bias is no match for thousands upon thousands of informed citizens. Just ask the editors of *Pravda* if you want evidence of that.

- *We need to make sure our elected officials do* their *homework—and then do* their *jobs.* We need to hold them accountable for both their words and their deeds. It is an old political maxim that only if our magistrates "feel the heat" will they ever "see the light." Calls and letters are important, but there are a number of other simple things we can do. We can attend town meetings. We can serve on feasibility committees. We can volunteer for campaigns—to walk a precinct or district, to answer phones, or to stuff envelopes. In short, we can make an enormous difference if we'll just become involved in our community. Participatory government cannot work if we do not actually participate.

- *We can put our money where our faith is.* In other words, we can exercise wise consumer stewardship. The companies that produce these human pesticides do so for pure economic profit. If the enterprise ceases to be profitable, they will cease to promote it. It's that simple. Thus we can not only communicate with the companies, we can also adjust our consumer habits so we can enforce our convictions economically. Simply put, we should not do business with companies which are actively involved in medical genocide. The makers of RU-486, the French company Roussel-Uclaf and its German and Kuwaiti parent corporation Hoechst, do a booming trade—more than six billion dollars a year in the U.S. and another two billion dollars in Britain. Their products include Trevira carpets (as well as fibers, fabrics, and apparel), Lasix diuretics, Claforan antibiotics, Topicort creams, Acclaim herbicides, and One Shot pesticides. It is crucial that we make wise investments with the resources God has entrusted to us—utilizing selective buying and even boycotts to ensure that even our consumptive habits honor Christ and His principles.

- *We can participate in a sophisticated stock market strategy that targets key companies for stock trading that affects their net worth.* Designed by a group of Wall Street professionals who call themselves the RCR Alliance, this strategy has already caused the value of Hoechst shares to plummet twenty points. Anyone who invests on the Dow can now use their capitalist skills in the battle for life.

- *We can remain informed on the issue.* The situation with pharmacological development literally changes on a daily basis. There are several organizations that can provide us with the most recently updated information:

Legacy Communications
P.O. Box 680365
Franklin, TN 37068

Advocates for Life
P.O. Box 13656
Portland, OR 97213

American Life League
P.O. Box 490
Stafford, VA 22554

Americans United for Life
343 S. Dearborn, Suite 1804
Chicago, IL 60604

Concerned Women for America
370 L'Enfant Promenade S.W.
Suite 800
Washington, DC 20024

Focus on the Family
Citizen/Physician
801 Corporate Center
Pomona, CA 91768

Human Life International
7845 E. Airpark Rd.
Gaithersburg, MD 20879

National Right to Life Committee
419 7th St., NW, Suite 402
Washington, DC 20004

Pharmacists for Life
P.O. Box 130
Ingomar, PA 15127

RCR Alliance
2302 Oakland Blvd., NW
Roanoke, VA 24012

- Of course we can not only utilize the valuable information services these organizations provide, but *we can be involved in their ongoing work as well*—with our time, our effort, our prayers, and our financial support.
- In addition to all of these actions, we can contact the manufacturers and distributors of RU-486 directly to let them know of our grave concerns and our consumer stewardship commitments:

Hoechst A. G.
Postfach 80-03-20
Frankfurt Main D-6230
Germany

Roussel-Uclaf
35 Boulevard des Invalides
Paris, France 750-07

THE CHOICE

In 1909 Theodore Roosevelt addressed the nation as President one final time. In that speech he spoke prophetically about the challenges we would face in the course of the next century. His words seem to ring even truer today than they did then—if that is possible:

Progress has brought us both unbounded opportunities and unbridled difficulties. Thus, the measure of our civilization will not be that we have done much, but what we have done with that much. I believe that the next half century will determine if we will advance the cause of Christian civilization or revert to the horrors of brutal paganism. The thought of modern industry in the hands of Christian charity is a dream worth dreaming. The thought of industry in the hands of paganism is a nightmare beyond imagining. The choice between the two is upon us.[11]

Indeed, as we approach this pivotal *fin de siecle*, that choice is truly upon us. Will it then be an *annus terribilis* or an *annus mirabilis*? Clearly, it is up to us to decide.

BIBLIOGRAPHIC RESOURCES

Ora Et Labora[1]

The important thing generally is the next step. We ought not to take it unless we are sure that it is advisable; but we should not hesitate to take it once we are sure; and we can safely join with others who also wish to take it, without bothering our heads overmuch as to any somewhat fantastic theories that others may have concerning, say, the two hundredth step, which is not yet in sight.[2]

THEODORE ROOSEVELT

I never had any faith in luck at all, except that I believe good luck will carry a man over a ditch if he jumps well, and will put a bit of bacon in his pot if he looks after his garden and keeps a pig; it taps at least once in a lifetime at everybody's door, but if industry does not open it, away it goes.[3]

CHARLES H. SPURGEON

THE research for this book included the work of innumerable writers, scholars, scientists, and commentators. The following bibliography includes only those consulted works directly related to the medical and pharmaceutical abortifacient industries. All the other book, pamphlet, monograph, and periodical sources are copiously recorded in the end-note documentation for further study and reference.

Ankerberg, John and John Weldon. *Can You Trust Your Doctor?* Brentwood, TN: Wolgemuth and Hyatt, 1991.

Banks, J. A. and Olive. *Feminism and Family Planning in Victorian England*. New York: Shocken Books, 1964.

Baulieu, Etienne-Emile and Sheldon J. Segal. *The Antiprogestin Steroid RU-486 and Human Fertility Control*. New York: Plenum Press, 1985.

Baulieu, Etienne-Emile. *Generation Pilule*. Paris: Odile Jacob, 1991.

Billington, James H. *Fire in the Minds of Men: Origins of the Revolutionary Faith*. New York: Basic Books, 1980.

Brennan, William. *Medical Holocausts: Exterminative Medicine in Nazi Germany and Contemporary America*. New York: Nordland Publishing International, 1980.

Cartwright, F. F. *A Social History of Medicine*. New York: Longman Group Limited, 1977.

Chase, Allan. *The Legacy of Malthus: The Social Costs of the New Scientific Racism*. New York: Alfred A. Knopf, 1975.

DeJong, Peter and William Smit. *Planning Your Family: How to Decide What's Best for You*. Grand Rapids, MI: Zondervan, 1987.

deParrie, Paul and Mary Pride. *Unholy Sacrifices of the New Age*. Wheaton, IL: Crossway Books, 1988.

Espinosa, Dr. J. C. *Birth Control: Why Are They Lying to Women?* Washington, D.C.: Human Life International, 1980.

Evans, Debra. *Without Moral Limits: Women, Reproduction, and the New Medical Technology.* Wheaton, IL: Crossway Books, 1989.

Forrest, Jacqueline Darroch, Susan Harlap, and Kathryn Kost. *Preventing Pregnancy, Protecting Health: A New Look at Birth Control Choices in the United States.* New York: Alan Guttmacher Institute, 1991.

Frame, John M. *Medical Ethics: Principles, Persons, and Problems.* Phillipsburg, NJ: Presbyterian and Reformed, 1988.

Fryer, Peter. *The Birth Controllers.* New York: Stein and Day, 1965.

Gallagher, Hugh Gregory. *By Trust Betrayed: Patients, Physicians, and the License to Kill in the Third Reich.* New York: Henry Holt and Company, 1990.

Glassow, Dr. Richard D. *School-Based Clinics, the Abortion Connection.* Washington, D.C.: The National Right to Life Educational Trust Fund, 1988.

———. *Omen of the Future?: The Abortion Pill RU-486.* Washington, D.C.: The National Right to Life Educational Trust Fund, 1986.

Gordon, Linda. *Woman's Body, Woman's Right: Birth Control in America.* New York: Penguin Books, 1974.

Grant, George. *Changing Lives: Practical Strategies for Making a Difference in Your World.* Franklin, TN: Legacy Communications, 1991.

———. *Grand Illusions: The Legacy of Planned Parenthood.* Brentwood, TN: Wolgemuth and Hyatt, 1988.

———. *The Legacy of Planned Parenthood.* Brentwood, TN: Wolgemuth and Hyatt, 1989.

———. *Third Time Around: A History of the Pro-Life Movement From the First Century to the Present.* Brentwood, TN: Wolgemuth and Hyatt, 1991.

Guillebaud, John. *The Pill*. New York: Oxford University Press, 1980.

Illich, Ivan. *Limits to Medicine: Medical Nemesis: The Expropriation of Health*. New York: Penguin Books, 1976.

Jaki, Stanley L. *Chesterton, A Seer of Science*. Chicago: University of Illinois Press, 1986.

Kennedy, David M. *Birth Control in America*. London: Yale University Press, 1970.

Kennedy, D. James. *Infanticide and Euthanasia: Myths and Realities*. Ft. Lauderdale, FL: Coral Ridge Ministries Publishing, 1986.

———. *Reclaiming the Media*. Ft. Lauderdale, FL: Coral Ridge Ministries Publishing, 1988.

Lader, Lawrence. *RU486: The Pill That Could End the Abortion Wars and Why American Women Don't Have It*. New York: Addison-Wesley, 1991.

Lammers and Verhey. *On Moral Medicine*. Grand Rapids, MI: Eerdmans, 1987.

Lifton, Robert Jay. *The Nazi Doctors: Medical Killing and the Psychology of Genocide*. New York, Basic Books, 1986.

Luker, Kristin. *Abortion and the Politics of Motherhood*. Berkeley: University of California Press, 1984.

Maddox, Brenda. *The Pope and Contraception*. London: Chatto and Windus, 1991.

Marshall, Robert G. *Bayonets and Roses*. Washington, D.C.: American Life League, 1976.

Marx, Paul. *Confessions of a Prolife Missionary: The Journeys of Fr. Paul Marx, OSB*. Gaithersburg, MD: Human Life International, 1988.

Medina, John. *The Outer Limits of Life*. Nashville: Oliver-Nelson Books, 1991.

Olasky, Marvin. *The Press and Abortion, 1838-1988*. Hillsdale, NJ: Lawrence Erlbaum Associates, 1988.

Provan, Charles D. *The Bible and Birth Control*. Monongahela, PA: Zimmer Printing, 1989.

Rothman, Barbara Katz. *The Tentative Pregnancy: Prenatal Diagnosis and the Future of Motherhood*. New York: Viking, 1986.

Sanger, Margaret. *Birth Control: The Pivot of Civilization*. New York: Brentano's Publishers, 1922.

——. *Happiness in Marriage*. New York: Cornwall Press, 1926.

——. *Woman and the New Race*. New York: Truth Publishing Company, 1920.

Scheidler, Joseph M. *Closed: 99 Ways to Stop Abortion*. Wheaton, IL: Crossway Books, 1985.

Scott, Douglas R. *Inside Planned Parenthood*. Falls Church, VA: CAC Publications, 1990.

Seaman, Barbara. *The Doctors' Case Against the Pill*. Garden City, NY: Doubleday and Company, 1969.

Shapiro, Dr. Howard I. *The Birth Control Book: A Complete Guide for Men and Women*. New York: Avon Books, 1977.

There are, of course, dozens of other excellent books on the issue of abortion that are certain to be indispensable backdrops for this complex discussion. A comprehensive list of those resources as well as a bevy of other helpful materials is available from:

Legacy Communications
P.O. Box 680365
Franklin, TN 37068

NOTES

ACKNOWLEDGMENTS

1. "With pen running on."
2. Theodore Roosevelt, *The Foes of Our Own Household* (New York: Charles Scribner's Sons, 1926), p. 149.
3. Charles Haddon Spurgeon, *John Ploughman's Pictures* (Philadelphia: John Altemus, n.d.), p. 137.
4. Samuel Taylor Coleridge, *Collected Wit* (London: Michael Barttles, Ltd, 1919), p. 68.
5. Trytram Gylberd, *The Bard* (Humble, TX: Vorthos Publications, 1985), p. 14.
6. "While there is Wichita, there is hope."

INTRODUCTION

1. "Look to the end."
2. Theodore Roosevelt, *The Foes of Our Own Household* (New York: George H. Doran, 1917), p. 132.
3. Charles Haddon Spurgeon, *John Ploughman's Talk* (London: Passmore & Alabaster, n.d.), p. 162.
4. "To God alone be the glory. Jesus saves."

PART I: BREEDING CONTEMPT
CHAPTER ONE: Paris in Spring

1. Theodore Roosevelt, *The Foes of Our Own Household* (New York: Charles Scribner's Sons, 1917, 1926), p. 3.
2. Charles Haddon Spurgeon, *John Ploughman's Talk* (London: Passmore & Alabaster, n.d.), p. 162.
3. "Pale death."
4. Roosevelt, *The Foes of Our Own Household*, p. 172.
5. Spurgeon, *John Ploughman's Talk*, p. 51.
6. Martin Le Varidin, *The Charms of the Continent* (Cincinnati: Laurel Grove Press, 1907), p. 67.
7. A kind of penal asylum for mentally ill criminals.

8. Norville Alliston, *Building the Great Cathedrals* (New York: Villard & Stockmul, Publishers, 1978), p. 34.
9. Alexander Schmemann, *For the Life of the World* (Crestwood, NY: St. Vladimir's Seminary Press, 1973).
10. Cyril Connolly, *The Unquiet Grave* (London: Beckner & Lloyd, Ltd., 1944), pp. 316, 317.
11. Jacques Prevert, *Histoires* (Paris: Guillaume Aragon, 1963), p. 92.

> I was there when it happened, by the Pont Neuf,
> Not far from the building called the mint.
> I was there when she leaned over and it is I who pushed her.
> There was nothing else to be done.
> I am Misery.
> I did my job and the Seine did likewise
> When it closed its fraternal arm around her.

PART II: *A BITTER PILL*
CHAPTER TWO: *Death by Any Other Name*

1. Quoted in David L. Johnson, *Theodore Roosevelt: American Monarch* (Philadelphia: American History Sources, 1981), p. 44.
2. Charles Haddon Spurgeon, *John Ploughman's Talk* (London: Passmore & Alabaster, n.d.), p. 165.
3. "The facts speak for themselves."
4. Theodore Roosevelt, *The Foes of Our Own Household* (New York: Charles Scribner's Sons, 1926), p. 168.
5. Spurgeon, *John Ploughman's Talk,* p. 167.
6. *Omni Magazine*, October 1991.
7. *New York Observer*, May 16, 1991.
8. *Ibid.*
9. Lawrence Lader, *RU486: The Pill That Could End the Abortion Wars and Why American Women Don't Have It* (New York: Addison-Wesley, 1991), p. 188.
10. *Ibid.*
11. From an undated fund-raising letter.
12. *Washington Post*, May 14, 1991.
13. Lader, *RU486: The Pill That Could End the Abortion Wars and Why American Women Don't Have It*, p. 19.
14. *Ibid.*, p. 20.
15. *Chicago Tribune*, July 19, 1990.
16. *New York Times*, October 22, 1989.
17. *USA Today*, January 15, 1987.
18. *Bernadell Technical Bulletin*, Vol. 1, No. 1, October 1989.
19. *Essex Right to Life Register*, Spring 1991.
20. *International Pro-Life News*, Vol. 16, No. 6.
21. *The Catholic Standard*, November 3, 1988.

22. Lader, *RU486: The Pill That Could End the Abortion Wars and Why American Women Don't Have It*, pp. 89-102.
23. *USA Today*, April 16, 1990.
24. *The Lewisville Sun*, May 19, 1991.
25. Those who reject or smash certain images.
26. Those who accept or revere certain images.
27. *Ibid.*
28. *Ibid.*
29. *The American Spectator*, October 1989.
30. *Ibid.*
31. *Chemical & Engineering News*, March 11, 1991.
32. *North Carolina Medical Journal*, 50:531-536.
33. *The American Spectator*, October 1989.
34. *Newsweek*, April 17, 1989.
35. *Dallas Morning News*, October 28, 1988.
36. *Fort Lauderdale Sun-Sentinel*, July 10, 1991.
37. *USA Today*, March 20, 1990.
38. *Fort Lauderdale Sun-Sentinel*, July 10, 1991.
39. *Life Magazine*, April 1990.
40. *Ibid.*
41. *Miami Herald*, May 16, 1991.
42. *American Druggist*, August 1991.
43. *Ibid.*
44. Uterine bleeding other than that caused by mentruation—often caused by growths in the urinary track or genital glands.
45. The measure of red blood cells stated as a percentage of the total blood volume.
46. Coronary or pulmonary distress.
47. *RU-486: A Diversion Attempt From the Health Minister*, International Inquiry Commission on RU-486, 1990.
48. *Le Figaro*, May 27, 1991.
49. *Ibid.*
50. *American Druggist*, August 1991.
51. *Ibid.*
52. *Lancet*, 2:1405, 1415-1418, 1987.
53. *New England Journal of Medicine*, 316:187-191, 1987.
54. *The British Medical Journal*, 290:580, 581, 1985.
55. *Fertil Steril*, 49:961-963, 1988.
56. *The British Journal of Family Planning*, 15:44-47, 1990.
57. *JAMA*, 262:1808-1814, 1989.
58. *The American Spectator*, October 1989.
59. *American Druggist*, August 1991.
60. Causing the development of physical defects in unborn children.
61. *Citizen Magazine*, August 1989.
62. *Concerned Women*, May 1990.
63. *Pro-Life News*, Vol. 16, No. 6.
64. *The New Republic*, January 27, 1986.
65. *Life Magazine*, April 1990.

66. *The New Republic*, January 27, 1986.
67. *Le Monde*, August 1, 1990; *Guardian Weekly*, August 19, 1990.
68. *Newsweek*, April 17, 1989.
69. *The American Spectator*, October 1989.
70. *Ibid.*
71. Lader, *RU486: The Pill That Could End the Abortion Wars and Why American Women Don't Have It*, p. 18.
72. *USA Today*, March 20, 1990.
73. *The Washington Post*, May 14, 1991.
74. *Pro Vitas Europe*, April 1990.
75. *USA Today*, January 15, 1987.
76. *Pro-Life Register of the Southeast*, June 1990.
77. *Citizen Magazine*, August 1989.
78. *The Washington Post*, May 14, 1991.
79. *Fort Lauderdale Sun-Sentinel*, July 10, 1991.
80. *Ibid.*
81. *Houston Chronicle*, January 14, 1991.
82. "Hard Questions and Straight Answers About RU-486," National Right to Life Committee, January 1991.
83. *RU-486: Substantive Therapeutic Usefulness,* International Inquiry Commission on RU-486, February 1991.
84. *Chemical & Engineering News*, March 11, 1991.
85. J. I. Packer, "Foreword," in Michael Scott Horton, *Mission Accomplished* (Nashville: Thomas Nelson, 1986), p. 11.
86. See Plato, *Great Dialogues of Plato* (New York: Mentor, 1956); and Thucydides, *History of the Peloponnesian War*, trans. W. H. D. Rouse (New York: Times Books, 1946).
87. See Plutarch, *Makers of Rome*, trans. Lou Scott-Kilvert (New York: Penguin, 1965); and Augustine, *The City of God*, trans. Robert A. B. Lawton (New York: Epoch Publications, 1957).
88. See Sergios Kasilov, *Icons of History*, trans. Vladimir Lloeslav (Paris: YMCA Press, 1962); and Basil Argyros, *Myth and Man*, trans. Cornelius Dolabella (New York: Caladea Press, 1961).
89. See Niccolo Machiavelli, *The Prince*, trans. Daniel Donno (New York: Bantam Books, 1966); and Thomas More, *Utopia*, trans. Peter K. Marshall (New York: Washington Square Press, 1965).
90. See Aleksandr Solzhenitsyn, *One Day in the Life of Ivan Denisovich*, trans. Max Harvard and Ronald Hingley (New York: Bantam, 1963); and Colin Thubron, *Where Nights Are Longest* (New York: Random House, 1983).

CHAPTER THREE: *The Holy Grail*

1. "Since the beginning of time."
2. Theodore Roosevelt, *The Foes of Our Own Household* (New York: Charles Scribner's Sons, 1926), p. 91.

3. Charles Haddon Spurgeon, *John Ploughman's Pictures* (Philadelphia: John Altemus, n.d.), p. 67.

4. Quoted in George J. Marlin *et al.*, eds., *The Quotable Chesterton* (Garden City, NY: Image Books, 1987), p. 34.

5. See George Grant, *Third Time Around: A History of the Pro-Life Movement from the First Century to the Present* (Brentwood, TN: Wolgemuth & Hyatt, 1991).

6. *Ibid.*

7. Faith Popcorn, *The Popcorn Report: The Future of Your Company, Your World, and Your Life* (New York: Doubleday, 1991), p. 1.

8. Cited in Alan Chase, *The Legacy of Malthus: The Social Costs of the New Scientific Racism* (New York: Alfred Knopf, 1977), p. 7.

9. The pseudo-science of measuring and redirecting racial bloodlines.

10. A eugenic offshoot that attempted to determine racial purity by measuring the size and shape of skulls.

11. See, for instance, Linda Gordon, *Woman's Body, Woman's Right: Birth Control in America* (New York: Penguin Books, 1976); and J. A. and Olive Banks, *Feminism and Family Planning in Victorian England* (New York: Schocken Books, 1977).

12. Emory Lasilovski, *The Radical Tradition* (St. Louis: Progressive Press, 1922), p. 35.

13. Michael Fletcher, *The Mark of the Races* (Atlanta: J. L. Nichols & Company, 1907), pp. 121, 122.

14. Quoted in Lawrence S. Pavilion, *Fascists, Marxists, Dictators, and Petty Tyrants: Oppressive Social Policies in the Twentieth Century* (London: Western Outpost Publications Centre, 1979), p. 71.

15. *Ibid.*

16. *Ibid.*, p. 96.

17. *Ibid.*

18. Margaret Sanger, *Birth Control: The Pivot of Civilization* (New York: Brentano's, 1922), p. 23.

19. *Ibid.*, p. 176.

20. *Ibid.*, p. 108.

21. See George Grant, *Grand Illusions: The Legacy of Planned Parenthood* (Brentwood, TN: Wolgemuth & Hyatt, 1988).

22. Lars Eddlemeyer, *The Quotable Anarchist* (London: The Progressive News, 1988), p. 39.

23. Margaret Sanger, *Sexual Happiness* (New York: Eugenics Publishing Company, 1926), p. 14.

24. Sara E. Rix, ed., *The American Woman 1987-88: A Report in Depth* (New York: W. W. Norton, 1987), p. 251.

25. Louis Harris and Associates, *American Teens Speak: Sex, Myths, TV, and Birth Control* (New York: Planned Parenthood Federation of America, 1986), p. 19.

26. Rix, *The American Woman 1987-88: A Report in Depth*, p. 254.

27. David Chilton, *Power in the Blood: A Christian Response to AIDS* (Brentwood, TN: Wolgemuth and Hyatt, 1987), p. 50.

28. Mark D. Hayward and Junichi Yagi, "Contraceptive Failure in the United

States: Estimates from the 1982 National Survey of Family Growth," *Family Planning Perspectives*, Vol. 18, No. 5, September/October 1986, table 5; and Melvin Zelnik, Michael A. Koenig, and Kim J. Young, "Sources of Prescription Contraceptives and Subsequent Pregnancy Among Young Women," *Family Planning Perspectives*, Vol. 16, No. 1, January/February 1984, pp. 6-13.

29. *Ibid.*
30. *Ibid.*
31. *Ibid.*
32. *Ibid.*
33. These rates are derived using the binomial probability formula of Robert Ruff extrapolating Planned Parenthood's published first-year failure rates over extended intervals. See Ruff, *Aborting Planned Parenthood* (Houston: New Vision Press, 1988), pp. 86-92.
34. *Ibid.*
35. *Ibid.*
36. *Ibid.*
37. Curt Young, *The Least of These* (Chicago: Moody Press, 1984), p. 30.
38. Paul Marx, *Confessions of a Prolife Missionary* (Gaithersburg, MD: Human Life International, 1988).
39. LeBeth Myers, *Women Around the Globe: An International Status Report* (London: Guyon Social Resource Center, 1986), p. 137.
40. Debbie Taylor *et al.*, *Women: A World Report* (New York: Oxford University Press, 1985), p. 10; and Paul B. Fowler, *Abortion: Toward an Evangelical Consensus* (Portland: Multnomah, 1987), p. 11.
41. Frederick S. Jaffe, Barbara L. Lindheim, and Philip R. Lee, *Abortion Politics: Private Morality and Public Policy* (New York: McGraw-Hill, 1981), p. 7.
42. "Celebrating Seventy Years of Service," 1986 Annual Report, Planned Parenthood Federation of America, pp. 23, 32.
43. "Seventy Years of Family Planning in America: A Chronology of Major Events," Planned Parenthood Federation of America, pp. 3, 8.
44. The myth persists that Margaret Sanger, Planned Parenthood's founder, was a trained "public health nurse" (as the 1986 Planned Parenthood report puts it), but that is patently untrue. See Madeline Gray, *Margaret Sanger: A Biography of the Champion of Birth Control* (New York: Richard Morek Publishers, 1979), p. 326.
45. "Celebrating," p. 14.
46. "Serving Human Needs, Preserving Human Rights," 1983 Annual Report, Planned Parenthood Federation of America, p. ii.
47. "Celebrating," p. 32.
48. *Ibid.*
49. *Planned Parenthood Affiliates, Chapters, and State Public Affairs Offices Directory*, 1984.
50. *Ibid.*
51. Sanger, *Birth Control: The Pivot of Civilization*, pp. 105-123.
52. *Ibid.*, p. 108.
53. *Ibid.*, p. 114.

54. *Ibid.*, p. 115.
55. *Ibid.*, pp. 116, 117.
56. See Gordon, *Woman's Body, Woman's Right: Birth Control in America*, pp. 329-355; "Ethnic Group and Welfare Statutes of Women Sterilized in Federally Funded Family Planning Programs," *Family Planning Perspectives*, Vol. 6, No. 4, Fall 1974; and "Low Income Task Force Report, Planned Parenthood: Objective 2000," January 5, 1987, Planned Parenthood of Houston and Southeast Texas.
57. Margaret Sanger, "Birth Control," *The Birth Control Review*, May 1919.
58. *The Woman Rebel*, May 1914.
59. See, for instance, Margaret Sanger's articles in *The Birth Control Review*, May 1919, May 1923, October 1926, and April 1932.
60. Margaret Sanger, "Plan for Peace," *The Birth Control Review*, Vol. 16, No. 4, April 1932.
61. See Erma C. Craven's eye-opening essay "Abortion, Poverty, and Black Genocide," in Thomas Hilger and Dennis J. Horan's *Abortion and Social Justice* (New York: Althea Books, 1981).
62. See Tim Zewther, for Planned Parenthood of Humboldt County, quoted in *The Union*, June 14, 1983; Martha Burt, *Public Costs for Teenage Childbearing*, Center for Population Options, Washington, D. C., 1986; and "Serving Human Need," *Planned Parenthood Review*, Vol. 3, No. 4, Winter 1983.
63. See the letter from Planned Parenthood of Northeastern Indiana board member Len Goldstein to *The Fort Wayne Journal-Gazette*, November 5, 1987.
64. Sanger, *The Pivot of Civilization*, p. 96.
65. Jaffe *et al.*, *Abortion Politics*, p. ix.
66. *Ibid.*
67. "Celebrating," pp. 22, 23.
68. *Ibid.*, pp. 9, 12.
69. *Ibid.*, pp. 9-11.
70. *Ibid.*, pp. 18, 19, 25-27.
71. *Ibid.*, pp. 9, 10.
72. "Serving," p. 4.
73. "Celebrating," p. 22.
74. *Ibid.*, pp. 10, 21, 27.
75. *Ibid.*, p. 24.
76. "Serving," pp. 14-16.
77. *Ibid.*, pp. 5, 6.
78. "Celebrating," pp. 3, 23.
79. *Ibid.*, p. 13.
80. *Ibid.*, pp. 8, 9.
81. *Ibid.*, pp. 16, 23.
82. *Ibid.*, p. 9.
83. "Serving," p. 13.
84. *Pro Vitas Europe*, October 1990.

85. Peter Collier and David Horowitz, *The Rockefellers: An American Dynasty* (New York: Summit Books, 1976), p. 48.
86. *Ibid.*, pp. 50, 51.
87. *Ibid.*, p. 52.
88. *Ibid.*, pp. 60, 61.
89. Marjorie Lawrence and Rufus Calahan, *The Rockefeller Dynasty* (Phoenix: The Voice of Liberty Press, 1977), pp. 67, 68.
90. *Ibid.*, p. 88.
91. *Ibid.*, pp. 166, 167.
92. Collier and Horowitz, *The Rockefellers: An American Dynasty*, pp. 152-154.
93. *Ibid.*, p. 151.
94. *Ibid.*
95. *Ibid.*, pp. 106-110.
96. *Ibid.*, p. 155.
97. *Pro Vitas Europe*, December 1987.
98. Hilaire Belloc, *Notes of a Curmudgen* (London: Albright's Ltd., 1956), pp. 42, 43.

CHAPTER FOUR: *Witch Doctors*

1. "The remedy is worse than the disease."
2. Theodore Roosevelt, *The Foes of Our Own Household* (New York: George H. Doran, 1917), p. 152.
3. Charles Haddon Spurgeon, *John Ploughman's Pictures* (Philadelphia: John Altemus, n.d.), p. 49.
4. See George Grant, *Grand Illusions: The Legacy of Planned Parenthood* (Brentwood, TN: Wolgemuth and Hyatt, 1988), pp. 62-85.
5. *Wall Street Journal*, March 3, 1990.
6. *London Times*, July 19, 1991.
7. *Yugoslav Praemedicatum*, Spring 1988.
8. Lewis Thomas, *The Lives of a Cell* (New York: Bantam, 1974), p. 35.
9. *The Guardian*, July 22, 1991.
10. *Ibid.*
11. *New Dimensions*, October 1991.
12. *Ibid.*
13. *Ibid.*
14. *Medical Socio-Economic Research Sources*, October 1990.
15. Lawrence Wright, *Clean and Decent: The Fascinating History of Hygiene in the West* (Toronto: The University of Toronto Press, 1967).
16. Guy Thuillier, *Pour un Histoire de la Iessive au XIX^{e}Siecle* (Paris: Annales, 1969).
17. Rene Dubos, *The Mirage of Health: Utopian Progress and Technological Change* (New York: Anchor Books, 1959); Thomas McKeown and Gordon McLachlan, eds., *Medical History and Medical Care: A Symposium of Perspectives* (Oxford, UK: Oxford University Press, 1971); John Powles, *Science, Medicine, and Man* (London: Pergamon Press,

1973); Rick Carlson, *The End of Medicine* (New York: Wiley Interscience, 1975); Jean-Claude Polak, *La Medecine du Capital* (Paris: Maspero, 1970); Willis Alan McDonald, *The Limits of Technological Medicine* (Chicago: International University Texts Symposium, 1988).

18. Derek J. de Solla-Price, *Big Science, Little Science* (New York: Columbia University Press, 1983), p. 121.

19. David Chilton, *Power in the Blood: A Christian Response to AIDS* (Brentwood, TN: Wolgemuth and Hyatt, 1987).

20. Heinrich Schipperges, *Utopien der Medizin: Geschichte und Kritik der Artztlichen Ideologie des 19. Jh.* (Salzburg: Muller, 1886).

21. Ivan Illich, *The Limits to Medicine* (London: Penguin Books, 1977), p. 23.

22. *Ibid.*

23. Robert H. Moser, *The Disease of Medical Progress* (Springfield, IL: Thomas Publishers, 1969); David M. Spain, *The Complications of Modern Medical Practices* (New York: Grune and Stratton, 1973); H. P. Kummerle, *Klinik und Therapie der Nebenwirkungen* (Stuttgart: Theime, 1973); Hermes Vallors, *Medical Malpractice* (London: Perrin Brothers, 1982).

24. *Ibid.*, p. 36.

25. Plinius Secundus, *Naturalis Historia*, 29:19.

26. Artificial sensory perception stimulated electronically, surgically, or photoceutically.

27. Carbon freezing and suspending of tissues or organisms for later use or resurrection.

28. Human software microchip implants for behavioral or sensory modification.

29. Bionic enhancements of organisms with mechanical parts.

30. Re-engineering of cell biology and organic structures.

31. See for instance the new quarterly magazine *Mondo 2000* for further information or documentation.

32. L. Meyler, *Side Effects of Drugs* (Baltimore: Williams and Wilkins, 1982).

33. Morton Mintz, *By Prescription Only* (Boston: Beacon Hill Press, 1977).

34. *Science*, 179:775-777.

35. See the excellent discussion of this issue in Debra Evans, *Without Moral Limits: Women, Reproduction, and the New Medical Technology* (Wheaton, IL: Crossway Books, 1989).

36. Barbara Seaman, *The Doctors' Case Against the Pill* (Garden City, NY: Doubleday, 1980).

37. John Guillebaud, *The Pill* (Oxford, UK: Oxford University Press, 1991).

38. *Le Figaro*, June 9, 1990.

39. Seaman, *The Doctors' Case Against the Pill*, p. 11.

40. *Dallas Times Herald*, January 29, 1989.

41. According to an advertising brochure for a Planned Parenthood professional's seminar on the insurability crisis: "A Risky Business," Spring 1987.

42. C. Everett Koop, *The Right to Live, the Right to Die* (Wheaton, IL: Tyndale House, 1976).
43. *Yugoslav Praemedicatum*, Spring 1988.
44. *The Business Outlook*, November 30, 1990.
45. John Ankerberg and John Weldon, *Can You Trust Your Doctor?: The Complete Guide to New Age Medicine and Its Threat to Your Family* (Brentwood, TN: Wolgemuth and Hyatt, 1991).
46. *Yugoslav Praemedicatum*, Spring 1988.
47. Barbara DeJong, *Tracing the Jewish Diaspora* (Amsterdam: The English Press, 1967).
48. *Ibid.*
49. Illich, *The Limits to Medicine*, p. 121.
50. See for instance the stimulating publications *The Journal of Biblical Ethics and Medicine, Ethics and Medicine,* and the *Georgia Nurses for Life* newsletter. For the best discussion of why medicine has lost its Hippocratic/Judeo-Christian worldview, see Nigel M. de S. Cameron, *The New Medicine* (Wheaton, IL: Crossway Books, 1992).
51. See for instance the writing in Focus on the Family's *Physician* magazine.
52. *American Opinion*, May 1958.
53. Brock Chisholm, *The World Health Organization Charter* (Brussels: United Nations Printing Office, 1955), p. 2.
54. *Ibid.*
55. *American Opinion*, May 1958.
56. *Ibid.*
57. *WHO Charter*, Article 19.
58. *Ibid.*, Article 20.
59. *Syracuse Herald-Journal*, April 29, 1988.
60. *Wall Street Journal*, May 9, 1989.
61. *Ibid.*
62. *Wall Street Journal*, June 19, 1986.
63. *American Opinion*, May 1958.
64. *Ibid.*
65. In a speech by Alan Guttmacher in 1969, he suggested that coercive measures would likely be necessary first in "India and China." Again, see Glassow's analysis in "Ideology Compels Fervid PPFA Abortion Advocacy."
66. See Stephen Mosher's important studies on the Chinese birth control atrocities, *Broken Earth* (New York: Free Press, 1983) and *Journey into the Forbidden China* (New York: Free Press, 1985). Also see Michael Weisskopf's articles that first appeared in the *Washington Post* and then were widely reprinted: "Abortion Policy Tears at China's Society" (January 7, 1985) and "China's Birth Policy Drives Some to Kill Baby Girls" (January 14, 1985).
67. Remarks made at the Planned Parenthood-sponsored Horizons in Reproductive Health Conference at the luxurious Hotel del Coronado resort in San Diego in 1985. See Paul L. Bail's analysis in "Planned Parenthood Speakers Support Red Chinese Forced Abortion," *American Life Lobby Issues*, June 1985.

68. Douglas Johnson, "New Battle Looms Over U.S. Aid for U.N. Agency Supporting Coerced Abortion," *National Right to Life News*, May 1, 1986, p. 1; and *Planned Parenthood Review*, Vol. 5, No. 1, Winter 1984/85.
69. Report to donors, International Planned Parenthood Federation, October 1983.
70. See, for example, *Newsweek* magazine's extensive coverage: March 29, 1982; July 12, 1982; April 30, 1984.
71. See William M. O'Reilly, *The Deadly Neo-Colonialism* (Washington, D.C.: Human Life International, 1986); *Planned Parenthood Review*, Vol. 2, No. 4, Winter 1982, p. 16; "The Facts About IPPF," The Human Life Center, University of Steubenville, Steubenville, Ohio; and "Serving: Performance of Projects Funded by Family Planning International Assistance in 1985," Planned Parenthood Federation of America.
72. "Report of the Working Group on the Promotion of Family Planning as a Basic Human Right," International Planned Parenthood Federation, London, 1984, pp. 21-23; and Donald P. Warwick, *Bitter Pills: Population Policies and Their Implementation in Eight Developing Countries* (London: Cambridge University Press, 1982), especially p. 64.
73. *The UN Report*, July 1986.
74. *The UN Report*, September 1990.
75. *Le Figaro*, October 22, 1988.
76. *Pro Vitas Europe*, May 1991.
77. *Ibid.*
78. *Omni*, September 1991.
79. T. S. Eliot, *The Complete Poems and Plays, 1909-1950* (New York: Harcourt, Brace, and World, 1958), p. 96.

CHAPTER FIVE: *The Glitz Blitz*

1. "In order to win over the masses."
2. Quoted in David L. Johnson, *Theodore Roosevelt: American Monarch* (Philadelphia: American History Sources, 1981), p. 57.
3. Charles Haddon Spurgeon, *John Ploughman's Pictures* (Philadelphia: John Altemus, n.d.), p. 80.
4. Quoted in *New York Times*, September 7, 1991.
5. Marlin Maddoux, *Free Speech or Propaganda? How the Media Distorts the Truth* (Nashville: Thomas Nelson, 1990), p. 13.
6. *Human Events*, May 1987.
7. *Ibid.*
8. *Ibid.*
9. Alvin Toffler, *Future Shock* (New York: Bantam, 1971), p. 155.
10. *Public Opinion*, October 1981.
11. *Los Angeles Times*, July 1, 1990.
12. *Ibid.*
13. *Pro Vitas Europe*, February 1991.
14. *Pro Vitas Europe*, January 1991.

15. *Carnaium UK Report*, September 11, 1989.
16. *Ibid.*
17. *Coral Springs Forum*, March 15, 1990.
18. *Time*, August 12, 1991.
19. *The Boca News*, September 10, 1990.
20. *Fort Lauderdale Sun-Sentinel*, July 10, 1991.
21. *Chemical & Engineering News*, March 11, 1991.
22. *Time*, February 26, 1990.
23. Edward J. Epstein, *Between Fact and Fiction: The Problem of Journalism* (New York: Vintage Books, 1975), p. 3.
24. *Ibid.*, p. 4.
25. *Ibid.*
26. Francis A. Schaeffer, *How Should We Then Live?* (Wheaton, IL: Crossway Books, 1975), pp. 242, 243
27. *Ibid.*, p. 240.
28. Tom Goldstein, *The News AT ANY COST: How Journalists Compromise Their Ethics to Shape the News* (New York: Touchstone Books, 1985).

PART III: *AGAINST THE TIDE*
CHAPTER SIX: *Fin de Siecle*

1. Theodore Roosevelt, *The Foes of Our Own Household* (New York: George H. Doran, 1917), p. 7.
2. Charles Haddon Spurgeon, *John Ploughman's Pictures* (Philadelphia: John Altemus, n.d.), pp. 24, 25.
3. "On the threshold."
4. Roosevelt, *The Foes of Our Own Household*, p. 47.
5. Spurgeon, *John Ploughman's Pictures*, p. 17.
6. Hillel Schwartz, *Century's End: A Cultural History of the Fin de Siecle* (New York: Doubleday, 1990), pp. 4, 5.
7. *Ibid.*
8. *Ibid.*
9. Thomas Carlyle, *Sartor Restartus* (London: Everyman Library, n.d.), p. 98.
10. Hilaire Belloc, *Avril* (London: Charter House, 1922), p. 11.
11. Quoted in David L. Johnson, *Theodore Roosevelt: American Monarch* (Philadelphia: American History Sources, 1981), p. 44.

BIBLIOGRAPHIC RESOURCES

1. "Pray and work."
2. A. B. Roosevelt, ed., *Theodore Roosevelt on: Race, Riots, Reds, and Crime* (New York: Roosevelt Memorial Association, 1939), p. 101.
3. Charles Haddon Spurgeon, *John Ploughman's Talk* (London: Passmore & Alabaster, n.d.), p. 48.

INDEX